THE THEORY AND PRACTICE OF AMERICAN MARXISM, 1957-1970

Richard Guarasci

University Press
of America™

Library of Congress Catalog Card Number: 80-1376

ABOUT THE AUTHOR

Richard Guarasci is a member of the faculty at St. Lawrence University in Canton, New York. He was a regional organizer for the New University Conference (NUC) and active in a variety of political activities during the late sixties and early seventies. He is the author of a number of academic articles and, presently, he is completing a book on worker participation and government regulation of occupational health.

Acknowledgements

The author wishes to acknowledge several authors and publishers for their permission to quote extensively from their copyrighted materials, among them from FALSE PROMISES by Stanley Aronowitz. Copyright (c) 1973 by Stanley Aronowitz. Used with permission of McGraw-Hill Book Company. Other acknowledgements are made in the text and accompanying footnotes.

For Carin, Bridget and Patrick

Table of Contents

Preface

Currently in the United States marxist and neo-marxist thought has been significantly advanced by writers such as Stanley Aronowitz, Herbert Gutman, David Montgomery and numerous others. Both the "new" labor history as well as the "marxist theory of the State" schools have made significant advances on the American radical intellectual heritage. One school has developed a theoretical perspective of the labor process which is founded on what Aronowitz has termed the "relative autonomy of labor" in the shaping of its own work culture and social consciousness. The theory of the State school of radical economists have sought to define the nature and limits of State power by developing the "relative autonomy of the State" thesis. Although major differences in theory and methodology exist between these two schools of thought, it is quite clear that each represents a major advance toward an "open" marxism more appropriate for the cultural and intellectual demeanor of the American experience.

While each of these schools are fundamentally at odds with a great deal of the critical scholarship presented in the decade of the New Left, both owe a great debt to that heritage for expanding the scope of critical inquiry beyond the borders of mechanistic determinism. For writers such as C. Wright Mills and Herbert Marcuse and numerous others, their main contribution was the rediscovery of the humanistic dimension of the marxist heritage. However flawed and politically vulnerable, their work reasserted the importance of the subjective aspect of the dialectical process, or what Mills, himself, more appropriately referred to as the connection between private troubles and public issues. It was their focus on culture in its most anthropological meaning which dignified the importance of their scholarship.

The serious "new" left writing in the 1960's was fundamentally devoted to understanding the cultural processes that fashioned the social consensus of advanced American capitalism. As we look back on much of this work we are struck by the obvious naivitee of its many assumptions but taken by the clarity and insite of yet other equally important premises. We find a great deal of the openness of today's marxist scholarship initially broached in these ideas.

The proposition that the political and economic stability of modern capitalism primarily rests on the strength of its cultural mechanisms, I have termed the New Left Idea. The one common theme of the serious New Left critics was the political importance of the cultural apparatus in the maintenance and expansion of American capitalism. Whether the topic was concerned with capital accumulation, imperialism or racism the New Left analysis centered on the process of consciousness formation for the viability of the capitalist state.

But theory always must be judged by practice within even the broadest of marxist paradigms and here the scholarship of these critics must be reconciled with its history. In this regard it will strike the reader that so much of the Student Movement of the 1960's had so little in common with the New Left Idea. Clearly no causal relationship existed between theory and practice. But like most intellectual histories, it is my task to define the symmetry of the theory and practice of this period as well as the incoherence of ideas and events. And there was so much of both.

The three principal intellectual contributions of the New Left Idea were initial analyses of what we now know as cultural hegemony, the nature of the state and the definition of class under advanced American capitalism. And while these terms would seem so foreign to the Student Movement of the 1960's, there were many pamphlets, articles and political strategies rested from movement documents that are sufficiently proximate to these categories for one to find some sense of symmetry between ideas and events, at least in random movements of that political history. Ultimately the fate of the Student Movement was determined not by the absence of ideas but rather by the correctness and isolation of the New Left Idea as well as the influence of objective economic and political realities. It is the purpose of this book to define the New Left Idea, assess the coherence of this body of literature against the history of the American New Left Student Movement and attempt a critical evaluation of this Idea for American marxist theory.

A number of my colleagues have read and criticized this manuscript. I would like to thank Bernard Morris, Leroy Riselback, Allen Ritter, David Sallich, Kenneth Dolbeare, Laurie Baron, Ansil Ramsey, Edward Magdol, Robert Schwartz and Charles Ellison. I thank all of them for their assistance and comments. Naturally all of the flaws in the text are uniquely my own. I also wish to express my gratitude for St. Lawrence University for several grants helpful in the completion of this work, with special thanks to Frank Piskor, Kenneth Baker and George Gibson. I will always be indebted to the hard work of Jean Deese and Sandy White in the preparation of this manuscript.

PART ONE:

THE NEW LEFT IDEA IN THE AMERICAN CONTEXT

Chapter One
The Genesis of the American New Left

The New Left Idea in the American context has been described in a variety of ways by a number of authors. Most of this literature reduces itself either to some form of a sympathetic justification for the New Left and the Student Movement or to involved treatises on the utopian character of the movement and hence its inevitable demise through self destruction.[1] A significant portion of this literature is composed of numerous anthologies of articles written by New Left authors explaining the movement and its "new" dynamics. A small number of works consists simply of chronological histories of specific movement events or more complete analysis of the period.[2] None of these works has drawn together the major American New Left writings and attempted to synthesize them for the purpose of identifying the New Left Idea in the American context. The purpose of this manuscript is to achieve that theoretical definition of the New Left idea.

This project requires an identification of the intellectual roots of the American New Left, an explication of the Idea in the American context, a description of the related practice and intellectual foundation of the Student Movement,

---

[1] Sympathetic treatments usually are written by past New Lefters: Paul Potter, A Name for Ourselves (New York: Little-Brown, 1971); Michael Lerner, The New Socialist Revolution (New York: Dell Pub., 1973); Greg Calvert and Carol Nieman, A Disrupted History, (New York: Random House, 1971). Criticisms are typified by Peter Clecak, Radical Paradoxes (New York: Harper & Row, 1973); and Gil Green, The New Radicalism (New York: International Pub., 1971).

[2] Much of this literature will be cited throughout this part and the remaining parts of this manuscript.

and finally an assessment of the internal logic and theoretical coherence of the New Left Idea. This part of the manuscript will take up the first two tasks and the final two parts will treat the remaining two.

Harbingers of the New Left: The Fifties, the End of Ideology and Bohemia

The Eisenhower fifities were dominated by the constant pronouncements of the closing of the ideological universe in American intellectual circles. With the exception of a few brave actors this period is best remembered for its stern demand for political consensus and intellectual conformity. Although the cultural hegemony[1] of this decade was in no way complete, critical thought and intellectual spontaneity were eclipsed by the technological society: the mixed economy, the pluralist commonwealth, and the consequent end of the ideological age. For the "Old Left" radical, the fifties were marked by the intellectual despair that accompanied the foreclosure of the political imagination by an apparent denial of capitalism's internal collapse and the simultaneous expose of socialism's failures. The generation of the New Left would paradoxically emerge

---

[1]Cultural hegemony is an important concept in Marxist and neo-Marxist theory and it will be consistently discussed throughout this manuscript. A brief formal definition is best supplied by Gwynn Williams: hegemony is "a socio-political situation . . . in which the philosophy and practice of society fuse and are in equilibrium; an order in which a certain way of life and thought is dominant, in which one concept of reality is diffused throughout society in all its institutional and private manifestations, informing with its spirit all taste, morality, customs, religious and political principles, and all social relations, particularly in their intellectual and moral connotations." Gwynn Williams, "Gramsci's Concepts of Egemonia" Journal of the History of Ideas, XXI, 4 (October-December, 1960), pg. 587.

from this decade that proclaimed the birth of a new historical epoch - where politics was to become irrelevant and simply administrative questions would remain. The non-ideological age was to be singularly concerned with the maintenance of the system's stability and the growth of its productive forces.

The thirties and forties were decades of political relevance for the American Left. The collapse of the Old Left socialist paradigm in the fifties was a result not only of the Cold War repression of critical thought and radical action but also attributable to the failure of Marxist praxis.[1] The social categories, the economic expectations and the political strategies of the traditional interpretation of Marxist theory were suddenly unworkable. After two decades of intense mass action, American Marxism was now without a following. Further it seemed an inadequate explanation of the complicated hybrid of monopoly capitalism. Accordingly, American Marxism was defenseless when confronted by the repressive onslaught of its political counterparts. Although political domination and cultural hegemony seemed complete to the generations of the Old Left, critical forces were at work during the fifties. William A. Williams, C. Wright Mills, Herbert Marcuse and others would inspire a new vanguard, free from the mechanistic traps of the old but also ignorant of their predecessor's experience, poorly schooled in Marxist thought, and destined to confront the absence of a theory of praxis

---

[1] Simply stated, praxis means the unification of theory and practice, of ideas and action. Theory, in and of itself, is an incomplete tool for understanding human behavior. Ideas and practical activity combine to form a unity in human behavior which is fashioned by the interplay of objective and subjective forces. The product is praxis. Marx speaks to the question of revolutionary praxis. For a fuller description of the subject see the following section on Marxist theory, particularly pages 19 to 47.

suitable for late capitalism -- a confrontation
that would constantly nag these new insurgents and
a confrontation that would ultimately define their
movement. For without a suitable praxis, the New
Left would be continuously tortured by its lack of
a political self identity and vice versa.

The End of Ideology and Rise of Pluralist Thought

The non-ideological society was to be
the new historical epoch which Western industrialized society was entering. The old ideologies, particularly Marxism, were not perceived as
irrelevant. The seeming virtues of a "mixed
economy," a burgeoning welfare state, and the rise
of an authoritarian Soviet socialism are several
factors in Daniel Bell's general explanation of
the loss by the old ideology of any 'persuasive
power.'[1] Bell stated the point more directly:

> For the radical intellectual who articu-
> lated the revolutionary impulses of the
> past century and a half, all this has
> meant an end to chiliastic hopes, to
> millenarianism, to apocalyptic thinking
> -- and to ideology. For ideology, which
> once was a road to action, has come to
> be a dead end.[2]

According to Bell the major questions
posed by the old ideology have been shelved if not
resolved. The working class was well integrated
into the fabric of advanced capitalist society,
and most importantly this class was content with
the contemporary social arrangement. The mixed
economy of welfare state capitalism was capable of
producing a sufficiently ameliorative benefit
structure blunting the previously harsh realities
of capitalist development. Modern capitalism was

---

[1] Daniel Bell, "The End of Ideology in the West: An
Epilogue" in The End of Ideology (New York: Free
Press, 1960).

[2] Ibid., pg. 393.

a stable social system. The great antagonism between capital and labor was resolved for this epoch. As Irwin Unger has written of that period, conflict was perceived by the "non-ideologists" as no longer dualistic but rather pluralistic.[1] Instead of the two main categories of capital and labor, the non-ideological era had produced an open class society and the political arena had become a market place for a variety of group conflicts within the context of a dynamic Welfare State. The administration of these smaller conflicts was the major task of politics, reducing it simply to the implementation of the policies of a pluralist society. The state would now rationalize the open market place of political conflict. Politics was the administration of this mechanism. Social changes were possible through the growth of the productive forces, the Welfare State and the rising standard of living. To paraphrase C. Wright Mills, the non-ideological liberal perceived the historical agency for change as the very institutions of pluralist society.[2]

Clearly the "End of Ideology" projection would be short-lived. By the end of the fifties and certainly by the early sixties it was quite obvious that there would be a revival of public political reflection. Mills firmly isolated the "end of ideology" as simply a justification for the political status quo, hence another ideology. It was rooted upon "a disbelief in the shaping by men of their own futures . . . ".[3] Somehow Bell and the other liberals, who so staunchly discarded Marx for his deterministic and mechanistic materi-

---

[1] Irwin Unger, The Movement: A History of the American New Left 1959-1972 (New York: Dodd and Mead, 1974), pg. 12.

[2] See two of Mills' pieces. C. Wright Mills, "Liberal Values in the Modern World," and "The New Left" in Power, People and Politics (London: Oxford University Press, 1963).

[3] C. W. Mills, op cit., "The New Left," pg. 249.

alism, constructed an ideology that rested on the assumptions of a new political invisible hand -- a self correcting pluralist commonwealth.[1] Finally, Mills identifies the liberals' "end of ideology" as an attempt to dislodge themselves from their previous radical identities. The status quo orientation, the belief in technology and administration, and the acceptance of the cold war assumptions were all hidden under the surface of 'non-ideological, value free objective scholarship.' In reality the end of ideology was based on the end of the ideological commitment of its respective advocates.[2]

The Beats and Other Rebels

Although the fifties were certainly categorized as a period of intellectual and political despair for the American radical and cultural homogeneity and social stability for the pluralists, there were clearly disquieting sounds of resistance. In addition to the movements against American imperialism and capitalist intervention in Asia and Latin America, there were enclaves of antagonism within the midst of American culture. As Carl Ogelsby has written, the American fifties were by no means devoid of forces antithetical to the growth of one dimensional culture. Important among these were the 'phenomenon of middle class juvenile crime,' the surfacing of the Bohemian Beats, and a growing cultural and spiritual uneasiness.

---

[1] Irwin Unger, op cit., pg. 12. Unger identifies a number of "end of ideologist," pluralist fellow travelers -- Lipsett, Dahl, Hoftstadter, Boorstin, Lazarsfeld, et. al.

[2] Carl Ogelsby, "The Idea of the New Left" in Ogelsby, ed. The New Left Reader (New York: Grove Press, 1969).

As Ogelsby explains, suddenly the old liberal conviction of the symbiotic relationship between crime and poverty was now obsolete. White middle class children were committing offenses against property and not for it. A confused public witnessed the anti-social actors captured on the screen by James Dean and in music by Little Richard and Elvis Presley. Somehow a social system solidly constructed on a materialist ideological framework was producing subcultures of non-rational rebellion. Indeed the fifties were concerned with the new 'rebels without a cause.'

The Beats were in many ways the extreme expression of this cultural resistance. Responding to what appeared to them as an irrational and absurd world where 'science fiction has turned fact,' the Beats sought not a confrontation with society -- as their counter cultural offspring of the '60's -- but rather they sought pockets of relief in the confines of a defeated subculture. As William Carlos Williams wrote in the introduction to Allen Ginsburg's popular Beat poem, Howl, "It is a howl of defeat."[1]

The Beats were attempting to disengage from 'the Gray Flannel America' of the fifties. Writing on the philosophy of the beat generation, John Cellon Holmes described the "real journey of the Beats as inward."[2] Their quest was spiritual not political. They portrayed their rebellion with a clear sense of fatalism and morbidity, quite the opposite of the early enthusiasm and cultural celebrations of both white counter culture and Black nationalism of the sixties. Liberation -- if any existed at all for the Beats --

---

[1]William Carlos Williams, "Introduction" in Allen Ginsburg, Howl and Other Poems (San Francisco: City Lights Books, 1956).

[2]John Cellon Holmes, "The Philosophy of the Beat Generation" in Seymour Krim, ed., The Beats (New York: Fawcett Pub., 1960).

rested with the inner vibrations generated by "his trancelike 'digging' of jazz or sex or marijuana" in an attempt "to free himself not exert power over others.[1]

And it was clearly understood by the Beats that total inwardness and nonconformity resulted in self destruction. The American fifties generated a society that was gripped by fear -- of the reappearance of past economic collapse, world wide wars and destruction, and other unknown calamities. While deferring to the political parameters of the one dimensional society, the Beats were challenging its ability to punish its 'apolitical' nonconformists. The fact that the Beats challenged anything in the fifties marks their movement as memorable. The political radicals of the forties were now paralyzed by fear in the fifties. Indeed, fear was the national mood. In writing about the Student Movement in the fifties Andre Schiffrin described the political atmosphere as charged with political paranoia. "People were afraid to join anything, to sign anything, to lend their names to anything."[2] The fifties were perceived by the system's champions as a new non-ideological age blessed with affluence and stability soon to be referred to as a post industrial society. Simultaneously the fifties were seized by social, political and economic fears contained at the individual level, sublimated and kept below the public arenas. Intellectually it was a decade of pluralist triumph and the eclipse of critical social theory. Resistance was left to the Beats and their juvenile co-belligerents.

The American Left was, for the most part, obliterated in the fifties. Politically,

---

[1] J. C. Holmes, op cit., pg. 22.

[2] Andre Schiffrin, The Student Movement in the '50s (New England Free Press, Undated).

9

organizations not movements existed. Public
activity was rare. By comparison to the two
previous decades, mass action was nonexistent.
Intellectually, the Left was deserted by many of
its former adherents. Faced with obvious challenges to orthodox Marxist theory, the Old Left -
which was for the most part the American Communist
Party - was unable to successfully defend or
revise itself.

The Communist Party, the major Left
organization in the United States since the
1920's, was totally concerned with its self
defense during the McCarthy period of the 1950's.[1]
Even it was amenable to a re-examination of its
social strategy and theory, the CPUSA was unable
to attend to that chore. The remaining Left
groups and radical scholars were faced with the
immediate threat of political repression and their
focus was on personal survival. The radical's
dilemma in the fifties was to remain true to the
humanistic principles embodied in previous decades
of movement and scholarship while simultaneously
re-evaluating and revising a dogmatic and mechanistic Marxist inheritance in a period of fear and
repression. The fifties radical was caught on the
one hand between an unsuccessful political analysis and its tired and worn out language that
promised only historical irrelevance, and on the
other hand, the direct threat of loss of job,
career, and safety.[2] The dilemma was captured by

---

[1]See James Weinstein and David Eakins, "Introduc-
tion" in Weinstein and Eakins, ed. For a New
America (New York: Vintage Books, 1970); Al
Richmond, A Long View From the Left (Boston:
Houghton Mifflan Company, 1973); James Weinstein,
Ambiguous Legacy: The Left in American Politics,
(New York: New Viewpoints, 1975). Each of these
essays offers an extended analysis of the politi-
cal focus of CPUSA in the 1950's.

[2]Weinstein and Eakins, Ibid.

10

the main character in Clancey Sigal's novel, _Going Away_. Ripped apart by the collapse of the American Left and the apparent failure of its social theory, Sigal's young man seeks refuge outside of American society. The intellectual and political contours of the 'end of ideology' are overwhelming.

> "The thirties had been my time, and I had been fourteen in 1940. The historic agencies of change are collapsed; and with them I. Why? I must find out."[1]

Initial Stirrings

Probably no one American radical better symbolizes the political and intellectual repression of the fifties, and simultaneously the transitional nature of this decade to American radicalism than C. Wright Mills. He was both the isolated neo-Marxist maverick of the social sciences and the intellectual catalyst for the emerging New Left. He was perceived as the "lonely and brave" intellectual signpost by the young new student leftists of the early sixties.[2] However, Mills was not the intellectual or political leader of

---

[1] For an articulate account see Al Richmond, _op cit_. and also Stanley Aronowitz, _False Promises_ (New York: McGraw-Hill, 1973).

[2] See Ogelsby, _op cit_., pg. 6. Also numerous descriptions and commentaries about the importance of Mills to the New Left are contained in the following: P. Jacobs and L. Landau, ed., _The New Radicals_ (New York: Vintage, 1966); Peter Clecak, _Ibid_; Unger cited above; Irving Louis Horowitz, "An Introduction to C. Wright Mills" in I. Louis Horowitz, ed., _Power, Politics and People: The Collected Essays of C. Wright Mills_ (New York: Oxford Press, 1967); and Kirkpatrick Sale, _S. D. S._, (New York: Random House, 1973).

11

the New Left.[1] It never became so intellectually sophisticated as to have one. A central concern of his written work is the construction of non-dogmatic and non-mechanistic social theory that is accountable to the contemporary world scene. Clearly this meant to Mills a thorough explanation of the collapse of the historic agency for change in the postwar world. In fact, Mills understood this to be the central political issue confronting the Left.[2]

Much of Mills' works illuminates the social uneasiness represented in the late fifties and early sixties. He spends much of his effort carefully detailing what was for him the unrealistic and socially removed foundations of both orthodox[3] Marxism and the contemporary social science. Mills openly questioned "the labor metaphysic" of orthodox Marxism that perceived the working[4] class as the necessary agency of social change. He also questioned the economic determinism of popular Marxism, as well as the naive notions of the "ruling class" that permeated American Marxist thought. He was annoyed that these remnants of orthodoxy penetrated the work of some New Leftists. He understood these concepts as obsolete "in the face of the really impressive historical evidence that now stands against this expectation."[5] In brief, Mills sought to re-

---

[1] An excellent early essay that touches on this point is Dale L. Johnson, "On the Ideology of the Campus Revolution," Studies on the Left, Vol. II, No. 1, 1961.

[2] C. Wright Mills, "The New Left," op cit., pg. 255.

[3] See among other writings, C. W. Mills, The Marxists (Dell Publishing Co., 1962) and The Sociological Imagination (New York: Oxford Press, 1959).

[4] C. W. Mills, op cit., pg. 256.

[5] Mills, op cit., pg. 256.

establish the historical specificity of Marxist thought. In this sense, his work challenged all the basic categories of radical political thought that serviced the political movements of the two previous decades.

The thrust of Mills' efforts was the construction of a social theory that explained the juncture of the individual's public interaction with the major social institutions and his common everyday experiences. He sought an explanation of the relationship between "biography and history." Mills referred to this conception of social science as the "sociological imagination."[1] By achieving this goal, social science could then explain to men why they suffer from feelings of isolation and entrapment -- in other words, social alienation and personal estrangement.

To Mills, the application of the sociological imagination allowed for the construction of a responsible politics. The new politics would focus on exposing the irresponsible character of the contemporary political structure, and, therefore those who wish to change society would establish themselves as the legitimate holders of political responsibility.[2] What Mills was seeking was a new neo-Marxist praxis. He called for a modern social analysis, achieved through a revival of the critical spirit, and for the use of this theory in the construction of a political movement that would bid for power.

In looking beyond the traditional working class, Mills sought not new agencies for change as much as new pre-agencies. He turned to "intellectuals and the young intelligentsia" that

---

[1]See the first chapter of the Sociological Imagination entitled "The Promise."

[2]See C. Wright Mills, "The Politics of Responsibility" in C. Ogelsby, op cit., pgs. 23-27.

and acting in radical ways."[1] In refusing to accept orthodox theory in explaining the enigma of personal alienation and public indifference, Mills' writings during the fifties express both the intellectual frustration of the Left and the beginnings of political movement. He sought unorthodox agencies and catalysts for social change and his political sensitivity led him to intellectuals, students and youth. Measured in this manner, his work is characterized by a sense of urgency and implies coming movement.

C. Wright Mills was not the only public actor preparing the intellectual breakthroughs for the soon to be born New Student Left. In England the New Left Review appeared in 1959, a merger of two new journals, Universities and Left Review and the New Reasoner.[2] Comprised of some former members of the Communist Party at Oxford, the journal discussed issues related to estrangement and alienation. Radicals at the University of Wisconsin, some formerly involved in the old CPUSA's Labor Youth League, seriously began to read the New Left Review. It was obvious to them that CPUSA and its allied groups did not possess a[3] relevant vision of socialism in America.

In addition this group was also influenced by another "lonely and brave" radical in the American fifties, William Appleman Williams. A radical historian, Williams' writings confronted the issue of American imperialism and its relationship to the dynamics of American[4] domestic politics. He certainly helped open the

---

[1]Mills, "The New Left," op cit., pg. 257.

[2]Weinstein and Eakins, op cit., pg. 5.

[3]Weinstein and Eakins, op cit., pg. 5.

[4]Probably most important of his work in this York: Dell Pub., 1959).

14

way between the cold war position of the liberals
and Soviet oriented American communists. Williams
based his analysis on the Marxist proposition that
the United States initially avoided serious economic and political catastrophe because of its open
frontier which allowed for the expansion of markets and resources. Modern America, originating
with the Open Door Policy at the turn of the
century, was forced to an imperialist foreign
policy for the continued expansion of its economic
base. With America's entrance into the nuclear
age, the costs of an aggressive imperialist policy
threatened world wide holocaust. Williams es-
poused a neo-isolationship foreign policy and the
installation of an 'economic democracy' at home.

Williams' influence as well as that of
C. Wright Mills and the New Left Review inspired
several Wisconsin graduate students and several
others to found a new American radical journal
entitled Studies on the Left. Among the founders
were James Weinstein, Lee Baxandall, Saul Landau
and Lloyd Gardner.[1] This group was aware of the
failure of the Old Left and the need for a new
American praxis.[2] The editors of the new journal
were aware of the need for an American socialist
theory that would serve a new movement for social
change. Their explicit socialist position dis-
tinguished them from another radical group at the
University of Chicago which went on to publish
New University Thought. There was an attempt to
merge the two groups but the issue of the precise
use of the words "socialism" and "Left" prevented
any mutual effort on one journal. Both journals
appeared.

In the fall 1959 the Studies editors chose to
attack the question of socialist praxis, although

---

[1]See Unger, op cit., pg. 19. Also see Weinstein
and Eakins, op cit., pgs. 3-33.

[2]Weinstein and Eakins, op cit., pg. 6.

it was not specifically identified in these terms. Their first editorial discussed the political role of the socialist scholar in the academic world. The editorial began with a criticism of the hidden status quo orientation of the conventional "objective, dispassionate, non-partisan" approach to contemporary scholarship.[1] Dispassionate research does not guarantee unbiased research but probably does guarantee an acceptance of "things as they are." Rather the radical scholar uses his obvious commitment as a source for renewed objectivity.

> "Because he stands opposed to established institutions and conventional conceptions, the radical scholar possesses an unconcern for their safety or preservation."[2]

The purpose of radical scholarship is to inform practice -- at some point in time. The radical scholar is not simply pursuing knowledge for only its own sake nor is the radical scholar pursuing certain intellectual curiosities for some private celebration of academic scholarship. Rather the radical is determined to question, directly or indirectly, the legitimacy of the contemporary social milieux. He hopes that through the process of disclosing the history, character and ends of certain relationships his efforts will aid in the creation of new proposals for social construction. As the last line of the editorial stated:

> "We hope that the radicalism of what is disclosed, as it increases and matures,

---

[1] Editors of Studies on the Left, "The Radicalism of Disclosure," Studies on the Left, Vol. 1, No. 1, Fall 1959. Reprinted in Jacobs and Landau, op cit., pgs. 90-94. Also see Weinstein and Eakins, op cit., pgs. 7-10, for some fine commentary on that editorial.

[2] Editors of Studies on the Left, "Radicalism of Disclosure" in Jacobs and Landau, op cit., pg. 93.

may provide knowledge and theory for the future growth of a radicalism of what is proposed."[1]

The emergence of serious unorthodox radical scholarship in the fifties aided in the birth of the American New Left. It established a unique identity for the new movement. Its purposes were the creation of a theory and practice compatible with the American experience. Although they did not discard the heritage of previous attempts in the socialist project, the New Left intellectuals hoped to avoid the old traps. As the fifties closed with the arrival of Studies on the Left, the growing Civil Rights and disarmament movements, and the revolution in Cuba, the social atmosphere reflected political motion and intellectual space. As Mills wrote in 1960, "The Age of Complacency is ending. Let the old women complain wisely about 'the end of ideology.' We are beginning to move again."[2]

The fifties were over. The despair and isolation of the Old Left would now be pushed aside by a new generation of Americans. In just two short years after the appearance of Mills' proclamation of movement, the Students for a Democratic Society would be founded and their Port Huron Statement would begin with an "Agenda for a Generation."

"We are people of this generation, bred in at least modest comfort, housed now in universities, looking uncomfortably to the world we inherit."[3]

---

[1] Editors of Studies, op cit., pg. 54.

[2] C. Wright Mills, "The New Left," op cit., pg. 259.

[3] Students for A Democratic Society, Port Huron Statement, SDS, 1962. Obtained from the Wisconsin Historical Society, Madison, Wisconsin.

The intellectual and political heritage of the next ten years would significantly alter the character of American radicalism. The next decade offered political opportunities and culminated in significant setbacks and mortal defeats. The intellectual contribution of the New Left, particularly the New Student Left, would re-initiate the project for an American socialist praxis. In this effort the New Left would offer some important new concepts to a radical analysis of developed capitalism. Many times it would fail to integrate its own analysis with New Left practice. As it will be cited throughout this essay, many commentators on the New Left have incorrectly identified the New Left's ideas and the relationship of those ideas to the New Left's political practice. Contrary to many contemporary analyses of this movement, the New Left would represent an important starting point for the resolution of what Peter Clecak referred to as "radical paradoxes."[1] The intellectual heritage of the New Left and the Student Movement present not a misguided attempt at Utopia, but a sustained attempt to answer Sigal's perceptive question: "The historic agencies for change have collapsed . . . Why? I must find out." Much of the "New Left Idea" brought us closer to an answer than the communist and social democratic answers of the past.

---

[1] Peter Clecak, _op_ _cit_.

Chapter Two
The New Left and Neo-Marxism

Interpretations of the New Left are more often than not captured by the particular ideological bias of the writer. There is, moreover, a built-in distinction not to concede the New Left any theoretical basis or coherence of ideas, largely, I suppose because of its association with hippiedom, drugs, erratic behavior, etc. At this point, it is not my intent to re-evaluate the Student Movement, but rather to outline briefly the major aspects of its practice, isolating the major junctures in its intellectual history, and explicate its contribution to American radical thought. So much of the literature on the New Left is either a semi-sympathetic chronology of its events and issues, spiced with heroic tales of political adventure or, antithetically, a more sober, although equally unsatisfying presentation of the intellectual efforts of the movement fixing itself solely on the utopian posture of various New Left theorists.[1] Although this literature is not without merit as important chronological work or as a necessary intellectual challenge, it nevertheless is insufficient as an appropriate historical interpretation of the New Left and Student Movements.

---

[1]The first group is best represented by Sale's S.D.S., although a variety of volumes fit this model. Among them Paul Potter, A Name for Ourselves (New York: Little Brown, 1971); Massimo Teodori, The New Left; A Documentary History (New York: Bobbs-Merrill, 1968); Jacobs and Landau, op cit. and many more to be confronted in this manuscript. The second group is exemplified by Peter Clecak, op cit.; Gil Green, The New Radicalism (New York: International, 1972); Jack Woddis, New Theories of Revolution (New York: International, 1972); and Christopher Lasch, The Agony of the American Left (New York: Vintage, 1969).

Perhaps the best history of the American New Left Student Movement has been written by Kirkpatrick Sale. Sale divides the political experience of the Student Movement into four discernable periods: the early period from 1960-62 as a time of Reorganization; 1962-65 as the years of Reform, particularly characterized by the Civil Rights movement and the organizing of poor northern communities; the early anti-war years as Resistance, 1965-68; and finally the 1968-70 stage as that of Revolution.[1]

Sale's organization of the events affords a clear demarcation of the actions of the Student Movement. As well researched and written as it is and with admirable regard for precision and completeness, Sale's account comes down simply to a chronological ensemble of events. It makes no significant attempt to evaluate the intellectual malaise that the New Student Left inherited from the Old Left or to measure the Movement's attempt to reconstruct a theoretical overview of developed capitalism in the United States. Although Sale's categories do help the reader conceptualize the various changes in the programmatic profile of the Student Movement, they fail to help the reader comprehend the intellectual tension that each period represents. Sale, like many other authors and editors, presents the Student Movement as simply a series of disjointed and controversial issues and programs. The weakness of this approach is that it severs the New Student Left from its political and intellectual roots. It presents the movement in an a-historical fashion, consequently losing sight of an important dimension of its experience. What is lost in particular is an understanding of the New Left and the Student Movement as an important advance in the continuing history of the development of a genuine American marxist and radical theory. It is true that the intellectual contributions of these movements were unsuccessful in answering

---

[1]Kirkpatrick Sale, op cit.

the crucial questions put before it, but these movements nevertheless redirected the theoretical focus of American marxism toward the cultural and ideological dimension of the everyday life experiences of the working class and related social groupings. Further, they attempted to resolve the question of revolutionary consciousness by asserting the existence of a link between a radical praxis and the political consciousness of the working class. The New Left assumed that the presentation of a revolutionary praxis that embodied not only a vision of the "new society," but also its very institutions, would provide the necessary breakthrough in the construction of revolutionary consciousness within the broader spectrum of society. The New Student Left can only be fully comprehended when its intellectual and social history is perceived as the unfolding of a new political project -- the construction of a new praxis for late capitalism; in other words, as the genesis of a new theoretical conceptualization of modern capitalism and the development of a workable political strategy and everyday practice appropriate to that historical moment.

The four categories that Sale employs in his history of the Students for a Democratic Society are more appropriately re-defined into broader perspectives. The period of Reorganization (1960-62) is better portrayed as the attempt to renew an historical political analysis embodied by Mills and Williams as opposed to the closed, static model of Bell and his liberal colleagues. The years of Reform (1962-65) may now be understood as the initial attempts in the search for a new historic agency for change and related political catalysts. The Resistance (1965-68) is better grasped as the search for an appropriate political strategy coupled with the continuing search for agencies. Finally, the period of Revolution (1968-70) is the capitulation of the New Left and Student Movements to the old strategies and structures. The result is its suicide caused by the schizophrenia born in the attempted merger of the old Leninist puritanism and the need for the new liberating sensibility. In short, the new movement's recognition of its failure to complete its project, and in fact its decision to abandon it resulted in self-destruction.

Conceived as political project, the New Left and its Student Movement are best identified with three major contributions that also help to define the New Left Idea. The first of these is the New Left's reassertion of the political nature of the cultural apparatus and its importance in the maintenance of non-revolutionary consciousness. Its intellectual contribution centers on the political identification of the institutions of system legitimization and their relationship to the creation and maintenance of system supportive values, and their penetration into the interpretation of everyday life experiences by the non-elite members of society. The New Left's edict that the "personal is the political" is clearly the popular framework of this concept. Borrowing heavily at times from the Freudian thrust, the New Left idea attempts clearly to identify the relationship between the political economy of capitalism and the development and structure of personality.[1]

The second major contribution is the initial development of a political economic analysis of "late capitalism. The New Left initiated an outline of contemporary capitalist society

---

[1]Three important works in this field of "Freudian Marxism" that clearly develop this point are Herbert Marcuse, Eros and Civilization (Boston: Beacon Press, 1956); Bruce Brown, Marx, Freud and the Critique of Everyday Life (New York: Monthly Review, 1973); and D. Howard and M. Klare, eds., The Unknown Dimension (New York: Basic Books, 1972). Anything approaching a complete bibliography of this school of marxist scholarship is beyond the scope of this note; however, Martin Jay, The Dialectical Imagination (New York: Little & Brown, 1973), will serve as a handsome introductory guide to the initial thrust of this approach as developed by the "Frankfurt School."

which is characterized by its (1) dependence on
the increased subsidization of capital by the
State in maintaining the growth of capitalism's
productive forces and ensuring its economic
stability; (2) mass production and mass consumption features in which its industrial and finan-
cial foundation is marked by its interlocking
arrangements and a severe concentration of economic power; and, (3) intensified cultural supports
which attempt the shaping of social consciousness
for the political and economic advantage of its
dominant vested interests.

Finally, the New Left began a re-inves-
tigation of the revolutionary potential of the
working class that included a search for other
agencies for change as well as the construction of
new historic classes. However, the question of
agency was cast in an enlarged vision of capitalist domination now necessarily depending on its
ideological, cultural and state apparatus.

In developing its ideas on the new role of
political control, the New Left and Student Movements were forced into an encounter with their
theoretical inheritance. The significance and
contributions of the New Left must be evaluated in
the context of its intellectual heritage in order
to satisfactorily measure its historical value.

Marx and "Orthodox Marxism"

In The Marxists C. Wright Mills notes
that, "The intellectual history of marxism is
characterized by tortuous and savage controver-
sies."[1] Any basic introduction to the history of
marxist thought elaborates on Mills' understate-
ment! For the American New Left the panorama of
radical ideologies and organizations reduced
themselves into two major camps by the 1950's:
the Leninist/Bolshevik school and the Social Demo-

---

[1]C. Wright Mills, The Marxists (New York: Dell
Pub., 1962), pg. 132.

23

cratic approach. A multiplicity of organizational and intellectual refinements were contained within each camp, but all could be placed between these two polar positions on the American Marxist continuum. Both of these approaches to theory and practice comprised the American Old Left that confronted the burgeoning New Left.[1] However, for all their strategic and theoretical differences, there was much common ground in the intellectual vineyard of the Old Left. For the New Left the important commonality of the various Old Left fractions is the dimension of Marxism which they jointly omitted.

This point can be better understood by briefly identifying the essential relationships of Marx's critique of the capitalist system, delineating the American Old Left emphasis and introducing the New Left and NeoMarxist revisions.

Marx understood societies as organized around the process of production. Although the ideological or cultural dimensions of society, including law, politics and religion, were important areas of human activity, Marx and Engels believed that these other aspects of societal interaction were cast within the economic framework of society's productive forces.[2] Within the productive sector of society, capitalist society established the crucial social and political relationships that would dominate the other significant areas of social existence.

---

[1] The anarchist and the syndicalist traditions were long dormant on the American scene by the 1950's. The I.W.W. and its anarcho-syndicalism genre had passed from the American scene. Clearly by the '50's it had no recognizable political profile.

[2] Irving Zeitlin outlines the key passages that pertain to this point: Marx and Engels, Selected Correspondence (Moscow: Foreign Languages Publishing House, 1953), cited in Irving Zeitlin, Marxism: A Re-Examination (New York: Van Nostrand, 1967).

Capitalist society is a class society ultimately organized around the owners of the means of production and those dependent only on the sale of their labor power.[1] Founding his analysis on the division of labor and private property, organized around the commodity form, Marx asserted that the relationship between classes is significantly altered under the capitalist system. Within the capitalist mode of production, the relationship between property owner and labor is organized around the buying and selling of labor power, itself, as a commodity.[2] Within this context the worker is paid not for the value produced by his labor but rather a sum which allows for a surplus. Although this surplus existed within the exploitative relationships under previous modes of production, the unique use of this surplus under capitalism differentiates this mode of production from its predecessors. Within the capitalist mode of production the surplus generated from the uses of labor power qua commodity is reinvested in the means of production. This allows for the dynamic nature of the capitalist system. Capitalism is a system based on the production of this surplus. As Marx wrote:

---

[1]Marx understood a bipolar class structure under capitalism as simply a tendency, emphatically stated in the last pages of Vol. I of Capital. "Along with the constantly diminishing number of advantages of this process of transformation, grows the mass of misery, oppression, slavery, degradation, exploitation . . .". Marx, Capital, Vol. I, pg. 763.

[2]Karl Marx, Capital, Volume I (New York: International Publishers, 1967). Marx wrote that labor is, ". . . a commodity whose use-value possesses the peculiar property of being a source of value, whose actual consumption, therefore, is itself an embodiment of labour, and consequently, a creation of value." pg. 167.

"Capitalist production is not merely the production of commodities, it is essentially the production of surplus-value."[1]

The worker now produces for the capitalist; consequently he not only must produce but he must produce surplus.

The production of surplus gives rise to capital. Capital is that part of the surplus that is reinvested in the means of production.[2] There are two kinds of capital. Constant capital is ". . . represented by the means of production, by the raw material, auxiliary material and the instruments of labor . . .".[3] Variable capital is ". . . that part of capital represented by labour-power . . .".[4] Within Marx's model, the capitalist mode of production provides for the continuing growth of the forces of production because of this "social" surplus supplied by the commodity exchange of labor power, serving as an uninterrupted source of capital. This new capital is partly invested into constant capital, adding thus to its initial base, the process that Marx identified as the "general law of capitalist accumulation." Constant capital outgrows variable capital. The dynamic growth generated by the capitalist mode of production and the accumulation of capital stimulates, "that change in the technical composition of capital by which the variable constituent becomes always smaller and smaller as compared with the constant."[5] The tendency under capitalism is therefore the continuous growth of the

---

[1] Marx, _Capital_, Vol. I, pg. 509.

[2] _Ibid._, pgs. 580-581.

[3] _Ibid._, pg. 209.

[4] _Ibid._, pg. 209.

[5] _Ibid._, pg. 624.

productive forces of society and relative decrease in the variable component.

Within this framework Marx outlines an extensive explanation of the exploitation and alienation of the workers, the non-owners of the means of production. Labor is exploited by the owner's realization of the surplus through the use of the market mechanism and relegation of labor to a commodity. It is this form of surplus creation that intensifies the exploitation and alienation of the worker. Marx wrote:

". . . the object which labor produces - labor's product - confronts it as 'something alien,' as a 'power independent' of the producer. The product of labor is labor which has been embodied in an object, which has become material: it is the 'objectification' of labor."[1]

Labor in its commodity form under capitalism, is estranged from the laborer. Put more directly by Marx:

"Political economy conceals the estrangement inherent in the nature of labor by not considering the direct relationship between the worker (labor) and production."[2]

Within the framework of the capitalist separation of worker and product, the worker becomes estranged or alienated from his labor. "It does not belong to his essential being."[3] The worker:

---

[1]Karl Marx, The Economic and Philosophic manuscripts of 1844, Dirk J. Struik (ed.), (New York: International Publishers, 1964), pg. 108.

[2]Ibid., pg. 110.

[3]Ibid., pg. 110.

"does not affirm himself but denies himself, does not feel content but unhappy, does not develop freely his physical and mental energy but mortifies his body and ruins his mind."[1]

Work under capitalism consequently is "not voluntary but coerced; it is 'forced labor.'"[2] As such labor does not satisfy man's creative instincts and needs external to it.[3] This estrangement results in daily activity alien to the human spirit, and ultimately in a "loss of self." Capitalism produces not only an estrangement between product and worker but when labor is projected into its commodity form it develops the "self estrangement" of the worker. Labor by its nature under capitalism "emasculates" the worker, forcing his creative instincts into an alien routine that demands a loss of self, hence an estrangement or alienation from self.

For the worker under capitalism, life is no longer an end but rather a "means of satisfying a need - the need to maintain physical existence."[4] For Marx life activity is labor in its free form. It fulfills the spontaneous and creative instinctual drives of man. But under capitalism, "Life itself appears only as a 'means to life.'"[5] Man is estranged from what he produces, estranged from his own body, his "external nature and spiritual essence." Alienated man perceives his real life activity, not as such, but rather as activity beyond his control and necessary for sustaining life.

---

[1] Ibid., pg. 110.

[2] Ibid., pgs. 110-111.

[3] Ibid., pg. 111.

[4] Ibid., pg. 113.

[5] Ibid., pg. 113.

Man's life activity is objectified or reified. But not only does estranged man reify his relationship with his work and find himself alien to himself, he is also estranged from other men. Man reifies his relationships with other beings because he has reduced life itself to a process - not an end - where he perceives himself as not the subject but rather the object of this process. As Marx wrote:

"An immediate consequence of the fact that man is estranged from the product of his labor, from his life activity, from his species being is the estrangement of man from man. When man confronts himself, he confronts the other man. What applies to a man's relation to his work, to the product of his labor and to himself, also holds of a man's relation to the other man, and to the other man's labor and object of labor."[1]

It is the exploitative nature of capitalism and its historically unique use of the source of exploitation - surplus value - that distinguishes it as a dynamic social system. This exploitative dimension of the system is also its source of strength and maintains the continued growth of its productive forces in unparalleled fashion. But this very source of strength, which feeds on this exploitation, rests on the rupture of man from his very nature. The extraction of surplus and capital from forced labor requires the worker's recognition of his powerless position in the production process. The worker perceives himself under the direction of uncontrollable and unaccountable forces, a creature subject to the domination of these forces and their masters. In short, the cooperation of the worker -- however enlisted -- is crucial for the continuance of the exploitative work relationship, which is the nucleus of the capitalist system. The internaliza-

---

[1] Ibid., pg. 114.

tion of the reified forms that surround the worker are crucial in prolonging this process. As Marx wrote:

> "Just as he creates his own production as the loss of his reality, as his punishment; his own product as a loss, as a product not belonging to him; so he creates the domination of the person who does not produce over production and over the product. Just as he estranges his own activity from himself, so he confers to the stranger an activity which is not his own."[1]

Marx outlined three forms of alienation under capitalism. Labor is disfigured and distorted within this mode of production resulting in alienation from the work process itself. Secondly, Marx wrote of the reification of man under the capitalist system. Man objectifies his perceptions of himself and other men. Interpersonal relationships are frozen in the alien milieux of self estranged beings, unable to fulfill their personal and social potential. Finally, the worker is alienated from the very object of his production, the thing produced. However, within bourgeois society he attempts to restore a degree of self identiy and purpose by accumulating those very objects produced. Money allows man to buy things which he hopes will aid him to be what he desperately desires but cannot attain in the reified form. As Marx wrote:

> "Money is the pimp between man's need and the object, between his life and his means of life. But that which mediates my life for me, also mediates the existence of other people for me. For me it is the other person."[2]

---

[1] *Ibid.*, pg. 116.

[2] *Ibid.*, pg. 167.

Within the context of bourgeois society money becomes the "universal agent of separation" for it appears to allow the creativity and definition absent from human activity under the capitalist mode. The owning of things potentially offers man the chance to be them. "That which is for me through the medium of money -- that for which I can pay (i.e., which money can buy) -- that I am."[1] The owning of commodities becomes a source of amelioration under capitalism -- or so it appears. In the end the "fetish of commodities" results in the continued estrangement of the worker as their real properties fall short of their desired attributes. The production of the commodity under capitalism which developed the worker's estrangement from the production process and his essential and spiritual nature, now completes its symmetrical loop. By serving to further alienate the worker through its false identification created in the "fetish of commodities", man seeks to satisfy those basic needs which are unsatiable in a society based on private property.

Under the capitalist mode of production the constant growth of the forces of production persist but so too does the exploitation and alienation of the working class. And Marx argues that within these contradictory tendencies the socialization of the work force is molded by capitalism's regimentation and descipling in which:

"The monopoly of capital becomes a fetter upon the mode of production itself . . . The knell of capitalist private property sounds.[2] The expropriators are expropriated."

In the interim the tension between the demands of the constant growth of the forces of production

---

[1] Ibid., pg. 167.

[2] Karl Marx, Capital, Vol. I, pg. 763.

and the weakening state of the exploitative "relations of production" is managed by the capitalist system. Marx expects the social and political consciousness of the working class to correlate with the development of the productive forces. Marx understands this as a tendency.

> "It is not the consciousness of men that determines their existence, but their social existence that determines their consciousness."[1]

He also realizes that the social fabric is a web of many human dimensions and that this fabric is bound by the capabilities of the material forces during specific historical epochs. This does not preclude a variety of political possibilities at any given historical moment. The mode of production modifies these structures and in part these structures modify social consciousness.

> "The totality of these relations of production constitutes the economic structure of society, the real foundation, on which arises a legal and political superstructure and to which correspond definite forms of social consciousness."[2]

The superstructure serves as an intermediary, adjusting the social structure and substructures to the framework of property relations and the given level of the development of the productive forces. Between the productive forces and the relations of production, this dialectical tension is bound by the limits of each as well as by the mediation of the superstructure.

---

[1]Karl Marx, Preface in A Contribution to the Critique of Political Economy (New York: International Publishers, 1972), pg. 21.

[2]Ibid., pg. 20.

The tension between the two eventually boils over and society enters "an era of social revolution." The alterations that occur in the productive forces' capabilities "lead sooner or later" to substitutions and changes in the ideological arenas, where "men become conscious and fight it out." The advances of economy and technology lead to developments in the artistic, religious, political, legal and philosophic structures.

> "No social order is ever destroyed before all the productive forces for which it is sufficient have been developed, and new superior relations of production never replace older ones before the material conditions of their existence have matured within the framework of the old society."[1]

The social system is built on the mode of production -- or base -- and the superstructure. The mode of production includes the productive forces (technological development, machines, the cooperation of labor, etc.) and the relations of production (formal/legal relations and work relations). The tension arising within the mode of production is contained in part by forces within the mode itself, but also by the ideological dimensions of the superstructure. In general, social consciousness corresponds to the historical possibilities generated by the dialectical tension and accompanying mediation. Marx is not saying that capitalism will fall by its own mechanistic resolution but rather he argues that 'antagonism' between the productive forces and relations of production will be managed but at some point,

> ". . . The productive forces developing within bourgeois society create also the

---

[1]Ibid., pg. 21.

material conditions for a solution of this antagonism."[1]

Capitalism creates economic and technical capabilities as well as certain historic possibilities and moments for human advancement.

The development of social consciousness leading to social revolution is a crucial area of Marx's work that is less developed. How consciousness progresses and how it is contained are not clearly outlined by Marx. However, he offers some significant insights which, when assembled, lead to a more developed construction of the problem.

The alienation of labor and its intensification under the capitalist mode of production doesn't directly correlate with the status of social consciousness. Although a positive relationship will be demonstrated at some moment of the historical process, particular oscillations in the former do not necessarily bring an identical response in the latter. At least Marx's writings do not state the relationship in this manner. Marx is writing about the tendencies of an historically specific social system; its various historical moments at any stage are simply that -- moments with probabilities attached to expected outcomes. In the sweep of the historical process Marx is confident of the superior influence of the essential variables -- the dominating weight of the human possibilities allowed by the development of the productive foces and its ultimate correspondence to social consciousness. However, particular historical moments produce opportunities, which may be modified by intervening factors.

Marx did not understand alienation to be an unalterable human condition but rather an historically specific artifact of social organiza-

---

[1]Ibid., pg. 21.

tion. Marx discusses alienation as a process of "inversion." The worker is "alienated, dispossessed, sold." The 'invested and inverted' processes of the capitalist mode require the dispossession of labor from the worker. Marx realized that other modes of production would be presented on the historical stage, available when the productive forces reached their appropriate level of development.

> "But obviously this process of inversion is merely 'historical' necessity, a necessity for the development of the foces of production solely from a specific historic point of departure, or basis, but in no way an 'absolute' necessity of production; rather a vanishing one . . .".[1]

As the capabilities of the productive forces develop, men can conceive of themselves as 'social individuals' rather than eternally 'private individuals.' Marx appears to be saying that the process of inversion begins to lose its ideological grip over society when men realize its historical obsolesence.

Marx wrote of the growing exploitation of the working class as inherent in the "general law of capitalist accumulation." The growth of constant capital relative to variable capital implies the continued expansion of capital. This growth is built on the decreasing relative (not absolute) share of variable capital and Marx projected an "industrial reserve" army of the unemployed as a complement to this "progress." In addition the dynamic features of capital yield a centralization of capital that results in a decreasing "number of magnates of capital."[2] Accom-

---

[1] Karl Marx, Grundrisse (New York: Vintage, 1973), translated by Martin Nicolaus, pg. 832.

[2] Karl Marx, Capital, Vol. I, pg. 763.

panying the growth of the productive forces is the growing,

> "mass of misery, oppression, slavery, degradation, exploitation; but with this too grows the revolt of the working class, a class always increasing in numbers, and disciplined, united, organized by the very mechanism of the process of capitalist production itself."[1]

The growing revolt of the working class is dependent on the development of its social consciousness. The class must become conscious of the process of inversion. "Class" must be perceived as not only exploitative but obsolete. The ideological hegemony of the capitalist system must be broken. Marx understood the complexity of this ideological domination and, one assumes, the complex and difficult process of ending it. In the German Ideology, Marx wrote:

> "The ideas of the ruling class are in every epoch the ruling ideas, i.e., the class which is the ruling material force of society, is at the same time its ruling intellectual force. The class which has the means of material production at its disposal, has control at the same time over the means of mental production . . .".[2]

As previously quoted, Marx wrote that after significant advances in the base, "sooner or later" the ideological supports of the superstructure would alter and ultimately conflict within the superstructure and would allow men to become conscious of the process of inversion and its his-

---

[1] Ibid., pg. 763.

[2] Karl Marx and Frederick Engels, The German Ideology (New York: International Publishers, 1970), pg. 64.

torical obsolescence.[1] What Marx does not supply is an analysis of the process of intellectual dismemberment and transformation. He does not state that the numerous and varigated economic crises which periodically confront capitalism will correlate identically with rises in the social consciousness. Rather Marx has implied, by an absence of specific correlations, a much greater subjective element is at work in this arena of consciousness and corresponding political developments. He thus leaves room for a less deterministic interpretation of the development of the subjective forces for political revolt.[2]

Marx's theory of crises extends his analysis of consciousness development. Capitalism suffers periodic crises due to its constant overproduction. The rising organic composition of capital, the increasing proportion of constant capital to variable, results in the decrease in the demand for labor (variable component) and the rise of surplus labor. Primarily because of the monopolization of capital and the declining rate of profit, the capitalist system "overproduces" or, stated in other terms, "underconsumes." Since the capitalism of Marx's time was devoid of significant state planning, changes in production levels and productivity rates, etc., in one industry were not necessarily balanced by appropriate adjustments in others, a crisis of "disproportionality"[3] was a constant threat to the capitalist mode.

---

[1] Karl Marx, Contribution to the Critique of Political Economy, pg. 21.

[2] No better exemplified than in Karl Marx, The Eighteenth Brumaire of Louis Bonaparte (New York: International Publishers, 1963).

[3] For a brief but direct statement see I. Zeitlin, op cit.

The periodic crises of overproduction or underconsumption are a regular feature of the capitalist system. However, this type of crisis is simply a crisis and Marx does not postulate that these "natural" workings will result in the final rupture of the system, sparking universal class consciousness among the working class. He never directly argues that the "pauperization" of the working class will independently result in the collapse of capitalism. Marx pursues the argument that relative proportions of wealth divided by capital and labor will historically drift towards an ever increasing share for capital. This position allows for increases in the standard of living for the working class as the absolute share that labor receives may increase while its relative share decreases. In sum Marx's theory of crisis is not clearly outlined as the negation of the system, but rather this tendency to periodic crisis develops historical possibilities and moments for the working class. These crises coupled with the progressive development of the technical and economic capacities of the productive forces under capitalism allow for certain political situations to occur. Ultimately the capitalist mode will give way to a new mode, but Marx did not project a series of worsening crises, which by themselves, in some suicidal fashion would bring on the socialist mode of production. Marx may have been at bottom a determinist, but never so vulgar or mechanistic.[1]

The absence of a complete political analysis of the revolutionary process by Marx apparently creates some confusion about the relationship between the transformations in the productive capabilities of advanced capitalism and

---

[1]Shlomo Avineri offers an excellent discussion of this point in The Social and Political Thought of Karl Marx (London: Cambridge University Press, 1968). Specifically see pages 174-184; also, see Bertell Ollman, Alienation: Marx's Concept of Man (New York: Cambridge University Press, 1971).

the growing tension developing in the relations of production. What conceptual bond weaves together the seemingly disparate threads in Marx's writings on the contradictions inherent in the advanced capitalist mode and the social consciousness and political activity of the working class? How are the contradictions realized and how are they exposed and confronted? Did Marx write about the relationship between the theoretical postulates of his critique of political economy and the practical social formations and political confrontations required for the dialectical transcendence of the capitalist system?

The crucial conceptual link in Marx's economic and political analysis is revolutionary practice which unites the subjective and objective elements of the historical process. It is through conscious political activity that the historical possibilities of the objective world are realized. The dialectic does not work in some automatic and mechanistic mode, producing social changes in the absence of meaningful human intervention, but rather,

". . . History is nothing but the succession of the separate generations, each of which exploits the materials, the capital funds, the productive force handed down to it by all preceeding generations, and thus, on the one hand, continues the traditional activity in completely changed circumstances with completely changed activity."[1]

It is the conjunction of the subjective and objective forces which shape history.

Marx rejected either simple materialist or idealist conceptions of history. He affirmed

---

[1]Karl Marx and Frederick Engels, _The German Ideology_ (New York: International Publishers, 1972), pg. 57.

the importance of practical contemplation in and of themselves determined the direction of history. Within the boundaries of the historical possibilities presented by the development of the productive forces, the unity of ideas and practical activity define the historical present.[1] This merger of theory and action is conceived of as praxis, which joins the political and economic dimensions of Marx's work.

Through praxis man is able to fashion various social and political formulas within the framework of the productive forces, and further, it is through praxis that Marx understands how the subjective forces define the length of the intervals between historical epochs. The objective forces produce moments and the subjective forces produce situations.[2]

On the one hand revolutionary praxis is concerned with the external conditions of the productive forces, the relations of production and the forms of mediation between each, and on the

---

[1]Marx wrote of Feuerbach's materialism: "The chief defect of all hitherto existing materialism is that the thing, reality, sensuousness, is conceived only in the form of the object or of contemplation, but not as sensuous human activity, practice, not subjectivity . . . Hence he does not grasp the significance of 'revolutionary,' of 'practical-critical,' activity." (K. Marx, Theses on Feuerbach included in K. Marx & F. Engels, op cit., pg. 121).

[2]Shlomo Avineri's comment is that, ". . . revolutionary praxis can realize theory only through the mediation of a passive element. This passive element is supplied by human needs that give rise to the possibility of realization. By themselves they do not cause revolutions - they make them possible . . ." [S. Avineri, The Social and Political Thought of Karl Marx (London: Cambridge University Press, 1968, pg. 139)].

other hand with the internal conditions that involve the subjective changes and self-realization (consciousness) experienced by the working class through political organization and activity. Revolutionary praxis -- different from capitalist praxis -- is the conceptual mechanism which retains the subjective element in Marx's political analysis.[1]

This position can be integrated with Marx's statement that 'ruling ideas are those of the ruling class.' It is revolutionary praxis, the unity of theory and practice, that breaks the intellectual hegemony of the dominant class and forges new developments in social transformation, allowing the working class to become conscious of its historical position and fashion its own world view. In short, revolutionary praxis is the link between Marx's "changes in the economic foundation [that] lead sooner or later to the transformation of the whole immense superstructure."[2] Stated in another manner, it is praxis which calls for the social consciousness that confronts the "twisted inversion" of labor in the everyday processes of the capitalist system.

Marx and the American Marxists

The American Old Left was intellectually dominated by a more stagnant interpretation and application of Marx's writings, utilizing his ideas more as dogmatic astrological projections rather than scientific concepts with specific historical relevance.

The American Left in the postwar era was composed of a variety of organizations, sects,

---

[1] For an analysis of capitalism as social praxis see chapter two of Henri Lefebvre, The Sociology of Marx (New York: Vintage, 1969).

[2] Karl Marx, "Preface." A Contribution to the Critique of Political Economy, op cit., pg. 21.

et. al. Each was wedded to its respective interpretation of Marx's writings. Trapped by the
absence of any workable strategy for radical
change, it was unable to develop an alternative to
the "Leninist" model, on the one hand, or the
"social democratic" strategy for evolutionary
socialism on the other. It dealt largely with
questions of political strategy but failed to
generate theoretical precepts responsive to contemporary American conditions. This is not to
argue that particular scholars did not attempt
this political and intellectual venture. The
point is that it never became part of the American
Marxist heritage because the primary focus of the
Old Left was on political practice.

    The Leninist Old Left accepted the in-
evitability of the "false consciousness" of the
working class and the consequent necessity for a
closed vanguard organization of professional
revolutionaries.[1] Marx's "sooner or later" proposition (on the eventual ideological and social
changes simultaneous with changes in the productive forces) was more likely to result in "never."
The Leninist approach assumes that a revolutionary
social consciousness is "brought from without."
As Lenin states, "The history of all countries
shows that the working class, exclusively by its
own effort, is able to develop only trade-union
consciousness."[2] An organization of professional
cadres is required to bring to this class a world
vision that encompasses the principles of Marxism.
The problem of "false consciousness" among the
working class is no longer a paradox but rather an
expectation treated by the vanguard antidote. The
American Communist Party - in all practical esti-
mates "The" Old Left since 1924 - simply tabled
the question by determining that false conscious-

---

[1]For Lenin's analysis see V. I. Lenin, What is to
be Done (New York: International Publishers,
1969), second printing.

[2]Ibid., pg. 31.

ness was alleviated by strategic and practical developments.[1] Assessments of developments within the economic and technical dimensions of the base and their relationship to the correlative ideological dimensions affecting social consciousness within the superstructure were relegated to the level of secondary pursuits. The question of consciousness was closed.

The social democratic thrust within the American Old Left "resolved" the problem of false consciousness with similar results. The evolutionary approach to socialism assumed that the reform orientation of its practice educates the working class about the virtues of a democratically controlled collective society. By strengthening the grip of the state over the market system and by urging the collectivezation of its failing parts, the state is deliberately closing the capitalist universe and allowing for the blossoming of the better instincts of civil society. However, the question of false consciousness is avoided by a narrow political concentration on strategic and tactical questions in the absence of any historical and theoretical context. Both of these Old Left approaches to the question of false consciousness failed to confront the intellectual weaknesses and ineffectual practice of the Left in the fifties; rather these two tendencies promised a premature end to the relevance of an American Marxist theory.

---

[1] See Weinstein's discussion of William Z. Foster, probably the most influential member of the CPUSA over a third of this century from the twenties through the fifties. When chairman of the party in the twenties Foster's book <u>Toward a Soviet America</u>, outlined CPUSA strategy where he clearly states that workplace political activity in conjunction with the overall programs of the Party will lead the American worker to follow the lead of their Soviet comrades and "abolish capitalism and establish Socialism." See, Weinstein, <u>op cit</u>., pgs. 48-49.

The New Left idea developed different approaches to the questions surrounding the agency for change, social consciousness, and modern capitalism. What made the New Left "new" was its approach to these questions. The intellectual contribution of the New Left lay in its attempt at developing an adequate explanation of the phenomenon of "false" consciousness, tracing its relationship to the sustained strength of late capitalism, and finally, suggesting new agencies for change or methods for revitalizing the old. Although New Left practice, and more particularly the student movement, was either ignorant or at odds with its intellectual brethren of the New Left, the significance of the inauguration of a new theoretical thrust within American Marxist circles should not be discounted. The New Left Idea was the initial step in the construction of a critical theory and socialist practice -- a revolutionary praxis -- appropriate for a Western developed society; the American New Left was a significant attempt to design a viable American Marxism. The practice of the American Student Movement of the 1960's in some aspects represents an important application and ultimately a revision of some of the New Left ideas. The two, the New Left Idea and the American Student Movement, must be studied together, because each in many ways defines the larger project -- the construction of a new praxis.

The intellectual contribution of the New Left to the development of this new praxis fell within three main categories: the concept of cultural hegemony, a definition of advanced capitalism, and a reassessment of the category of class. The question of false consciousness and more generally, consciousness development, is a central question to the American New Left. Social consciousness is significantly related to the expansive influence of the modern superstructure of advanced capitalism and the total social environment of the individual. The American New Left defined the entire ideological or cultural dimension as the arena of social consciousness. However, Marx's fundamental materialist assumptions remain intact, as do the social and politi-

cal character of the economic domain. More specifically the sociological and hierarchial relationships that are supportive of the dominant mode of
production. This mode requires compatible social
relationships in the individual's everyday life.
In short, the New Left approached the question of
consciousness development within the general
category of "capitalist cultural hegemony and the
critique of everyday life."

The second aspect of the New Left Idea
focused on the role of the state under modern
capitalism. The New Left in the United States was
significantly concerned with the fundamental
alterations within the base of the developed
capitalist system. It assessed the capacity of
the productive forces of late capitalism as well
as the concurrent changes within the supportive
superstructure. The thrust of this assessment led
the New Left to assert that the technological and
economic developments of late capitalism had
developed the capacity for the inauguration of a
post scarcity society; that is, the economic
capabilities of contemporary American capitalism
themselves allowed for the solution to the problems of material want and economic scarcity.
However the New Left never assumed that capitalism
could achieve a post scarcity status because the
very nature of capitalism demands an unequal
distribution of income. The New Left analysis
attempted to account for the dynamics of contemporary political economy that sustained present
day capitalism, specifying the role of the State
as a crucial factor in the maintenance of the
system, but failing to work out revolutionary
alternatives.

Finally, the New Left approached the
above questions with regard to their implications
for Marx's 'historic' agency for change. In fact,
a chronological history of the New Left would
originate with this question. The American Left,
always 'practically' oriented, was prone to advances in the strategic and tactical arenas in a
fashion that not only preceded theoretical development but many times precluded it. The American

New Left offered a variety of positions in the question of agency. In general it presented several surrogate agencies in place of the industrial working class, and ultimately moved in direction of new definitions of class and an overall synthesis. For simplicity, these questions will be categorized under the "question of agency."

The New Left and its Student Movement never identified their practice or related theoretical work in anything like the above categories. The Student Movement was burdened by anti-intellectualism that at every major point in its concentrated but popular history was to aggravate its inability to resolve major political questions. What is crucial to the continuing development of an American marxist theory is an accurate understanding of the New Left. The offhanded dismissal of the obvious failure of the Student Movement in building and maintaining viable political organizations and a responsible political program does not accomplish this.[1] The theoretical concerns and innovations of the New Left must be challenged and assessed. The characterization of the intellectual thrust and political actions of the New Left as utopian impossibilities, "exchanging the broken promises of socialism for illusions of communism" similarly does not adequately identify the historical intellectual breakthrough that the New Left Idea and the Student Movement represent.[2] An appropriate historical definition of the New Left must attempt to place its intellectual contribution within the context of the Old Left "paradoxes" and then assess the future relevance of the New Left Idea to the development of an American Marxist theory. To fall short of this task is to judge the New Left simply on its political performance and once again fall prey to the real paradox of the American Left -- its constant

---

[1] Gil Green, op cit., and Lasch, op cit.

[2] Clecak, op cit., pg. 30.

singular focus on the narrow realm of political practice.[1] Finally, to fully explicate the New Left Idea and its contribution to theory through its development of these three main categories of questions, an overview of the neo-marxist theoretical foundation of each category and the New Left application must be presented.

Cultural hegemony is concerned with the politics of culture and the relationship between what Marx defined as the mode of production and the consequent ideological social and ethical values which this mode requires.

In practice and theory the American New Left became obsessed with an investigation of this relationship within the modern parameters of twentieth century capitalism. A chronological history of this intellectual interest somehow misses the juncture between the theory and practice of the New Left. C. Wright Mills and Herbert Marcuse both provided major theoretical breakthroughs for the development of the New Left focus on culture and politics; however, since Mills' work was popularized previous to Marcuse's, the American New Left Idea originates with Mills' writing and then proceeds towards Marcuse's "Freudian Marxism."

Mills and the Politics of Culture

C. Wright Mills wrote extensively on the question of social consciousness. The topic creeps into almost all his major pieces, as if the author were unable to personally resolve the modern paradox of material affluence and social uneasiness. Mill's writing is characterized by a healthy degree of theoretical abstraction and precision joined by a sense of outrage and passion about contemporary social issues.

Mills consistently wrote of the feelings of uneasiness that dominated social consciousness

---

[1]Clecak's use of the term "radical paradoxes" and his overall analysis will be treated in a more complete manner in other sections of this chapter.

in the fifties: "Nowadays men often feel that
their private lives are a series of traps."[1] Men
were not only aware of being trapped within rigid
social categories but they were also aware of
their inability to transcend this condition. As
Mills wrote:

> "They sense that within their everyday
> worlds, they cannot overcome their
> troubles, and in this feeling, they are
> often quite correct . . .":[2]

Here Mills identified the problem of individual
estrangement, the growing awareness by individuals
of the objectification of their immediate milieux.
Mills described the emergence of this political
condition - the understanding that within contemporary society the individual is not the subject of his own biography. As Mills stated:

> "What ordinary men are directly aware of
> and what they try to do are bounded by
> the private orbits in which they live;
> their visions and their powers are
> limited to the close-up scenes of job,
> family, neighborhood . . .".[3]

Mills approached the question of consciousness and the growing uneasiness from the
perspective of the individual but within the
framework of the individual's immediate environment, his everyday life. He identifies the
limitations of contemporary social conscousness
and its exclusive concern with the private. The
perception of the separation of the public or
social domain from the private everyday life of
the individual is now in fact a description of

---

[1]C. Wright Mills, The Sociological Imagination,
pg. 3.

[2]Ibid., pg. 3.

[3]Ibid., pg. 3.

the undeveloped nature of contemporary social consciousness. And it is this very separation of public and private to which individual conciousness succumbs that sustains the growing uneasiness. While individuals are essentially spectators in the historical process,

> "the more aware they become, however vaguely, of ambitions and of threats which transcend their immediate locales, the more trapped they seem to feel."[1]

In short, men perceive their lives as separated from the major social institutions and the distant realms of elite power, but somehow they sense that this public domain affects their individual lives in some hidden manner. This sense of the undefined unrecognizable relationship between the great historical institutions and the private biography of the individual is the source of social uneasiness.

> ". . . men do not usually define the troubles they endure in terms of historical change and institutional contradiction."[2]

These individuals have internalized their lack of political influence in the historical process. "The very shaping of history now outpaces the ability of men to orient themselves in accordance with cherished values."[3] By implication Mills is contending that in the absence of the ability to control or significantly influence history, one can only dominate and protect his private orbit. Within the context of this social analysis, the separation of the public realm from that of the

---

[1]Ibid., pg. 3.

[2]Ibid., pg. 3.

[3]Ibid., pg. 4.

everyday life of the private citizen is quite rational - at least within the context of Mills' formulation. With the collapse of the old order and with it the 'cherished values,' coupled with the uncertainty of what history and the history-makers will design for future orders, the privation or fragmentation of experience should be expected within an era of social uneasiness. From Mills' framework one could argue that personal survival will not permit a merger of personal troubles and public issues when the nature of this relationship and the criteria for assessing it are undeveloped; that is, until the birth of a popular social theory or public philosophy that details the relationship between history and biography, social consciousness illuminating the contradictions of an advanced capitalist society will remain undeveloped. What will bring about change is what Mills described as the "sociological imagination."

> "It [the sociological imagination] is not merely one quality of mind among the contemporary range of cultural sensibilities - it is the quality whose wider and more adroit use offers the promise that all such sensibilities - and in fact, human reason itself - will come to play a greater role in human affairs."[1]

Mill's sociological imagination is analogous to the concept of a new praxis.

Mills asserted that liberalism was losing its credibility as a public philosophy and this was due essentially to the advancement of the economic and technical dimensions of society. In Marxist terminology, Mills maintained that the growth of the productive forces was causing changes in the relations of production and these alterations were simultaneously rendering obsolete

---

[1]Ibid., pg. 15.

the established relationships of the cultural and ideological arenas. The decaying order was magnifying the contradictions of capitalist society. More specifically, the private troubles encountered by individuals were directly related to the public issues of this society. Mills was seeking an explanation of this relationship and with it a vision of a more humane social order where reason would play a more vital role in the arrangement of the social fabric. This undefined world vision, coupled with an attempt at its realization, is a close approximation of Marx's praxis. In short, Mill's argument was a call for a new praxis that would bridge the gap between the institutional and personal domains. He sought a praxis that specifically focused on the everyday life of the individual as well as the broader public arena, linking each to the other.

Mills asserted that in fact the public and private arenas do overlap. The major public issues of the day and powerful elites do make history - and they are quite aware of it. Stripped of any individual influence in the historical process, the mass, the non-elites, separate these two arenas. For reasons of personal survival public experience is segregated from private life. One can go beyond Mills and state that it is mass consciousness which is "false," or at least realistic about personal political influence and individual happiness - but elite consciousness has no such illusions about the overlap of public and private domains of human experience. Elites have a "class" consciousness.

> "Nowhere in America is there as great a 'class consciousness' as among the elite; nowhere is it organized as effectively as among the power elite."[1]

---

[1]C. Wright Mills, <u>The Power Elite</u> (New York: Oxford University Press, 1959), pg. 283.

Within the context of Marxist theory the new praxis, or Mills' sociological imagination, must take hold among the "non elites." It is within this world that false perceptions, values, and interpretations of human experience are abundant. One major source of this "false" consciousness is the cultural part of the superstructure, whose role it is to develop the ideological support in the maintenance of the capitalist order. Analogous to Marx's cultural domination, Mills termed this ideological dimension the "cultural apparatus."

The life of the non-elites is greater than their immediate experience. "The quality of their lives is determined by meanings they have received from others."[1] The world of the non-elite is filled with interpretations of events, the introduction of and socialization to the dominant value system, and the translation of the meanings of current and past events. In general, the entire realm of culture is dramatically shaped by forces beyond the direct control of the individual, and Mills clearly understood this when he wrote:

"But in their everyday life they do not experience a world of solid fact; their experience itself is selected by stereotyped meanings and shaped by ready made interpretations."[2]

Their world view is not simply a function of their experience but rather their cultural perceptions are significantly framed by the ideological interpretations of the historical process wich are continuously being presented by the cultural apparatus.

---

[1] C. Wright Mills, "The Cultural Apparatus," in Power, Politics and People, op cit., pg. 405.

[2] Ibid., pg. 405.

Mills firmly contests a crucial assertion of Marx that material existence determines consciousness. Instead Mills argues that neither material existence nor social consciousness independently determines the other, but rather

> "Between consciousness and existence stand meanings and designs and communications which other men have passed on - first, in human speech itself, and later, by the management of symbols. These received and manipulated interpretations decisively influence such consciousness as men have of their existence."[1]

To Mills base does not determine superstructure or vice versa, nor does existence determine ideas. The economic or material realm is determinate, and simultaneously determined by the ideological cultural domain of the social system. In particular, the culture apparatus - the managing agent of interpretations of experience - shapes consciousness with the same level of significance as the material forces of society. One implication of Mills argument is that "false consciousness could be a direct result of the political or ideological role of the cultural apparatus. The cultural domain could disguise, blunt or mystify the social contradictions of advanced capitalism, consequently distorting social consciousness.

To Mills the cultural apparatus encompasses a variety of cultural arenas and an extensive "set of institutions." It is:

> "composed of all the organizations and milieux in which artistic, intellectual, and scientific work goes on, and of the means by which such work is made available to circles, publics and masses."[1]

---

[1]Ibid., pg. 405.

[2]Ibid., pg. 406.

Among others it includes the institutions of education, journalism, electronic media, theatre, film and art. According to Mills these institutions define the worlds in which men live by shaping the symbols and images of events as well as their general meanings. The general social environment and its relationship to individuals is dramatically influenced by the cultural apparatus. According to Marx social consciousness is partly formed by the ideological realms "in which men become conscious" of the inherent contradictions of capitalist society "and fight it out."[1] Mills is proposing that the cultural apparatus may negate this development. It is a matter of the relative power of the superstructure and the base.

The existence of the cultural apparatus and the centrality of its social position as a legitimizing agent for the social status quo fundamentally mark the social distance between individuals and social structure, or in Mills' terms, between personal biography and history. Men are now more than ever spectators in the historical process. They are dependent on the dominant social forces that shape history and explain the meaning and significance of events. The spectacles of the public domain are to be interpreted by the cultural agents previous to the individual's absorption of their existence and significance. As Mills wrote:

> "so decisive to experience itself are the results of these communications that often men do not really believe what 'they see before their very eyes' until they have been 'informed' about it by the national broadcast, the definitive book, the closeup photograph, the official announcement."[2]

---

[1] K. Marx, A Contribution to the Critique of Political Economy, pg. 21.

[2] Mills, op cit., pg. 407.

55

Mills is implying that all meaningful experience is public; that is, all significant experiences are parts of the greater spectacles of the cultural apparatus. Private experience is separate, less meaningful. In addition:

> "the cultural apparatus not only guides experience; often as well it expropriates the very chance to have experience that can rightly be called 'our own.'"[1]

To Mills the politics of culture rests on the relationship between the cultural apparatus and vested interest; that is, in the main, the cultural apparatus produces a consistant ideological thrust - it offers a range of system supportive and legitimizing values, ethics and stereotypes. The cultural apparatus consciously and unconsciously serves the interests of the dominant political forces of the contemporary status quo. The individual cultural workman's political ideology may be at odds with the ideological, and hence historical, role that the cultural apparatus performs in developed society.

> "The political choices of individuals must be distinguished from the political functions, uses and consequence of the cultural work they do."[2]

Within a marxist context the central social role of the cultural apparatus is the maintenance and expansion of a world view conducive to the parallel growth of the productive forces of developed society. This directly serves the vested interests of the dominant political and economic forces of that society such that the political implications of the cultural domain provide the ideological insulation for the elites. In short, de-

---

[1]<u>Ibid.</u>, pg. 407.

[2]<u>Ibid.</u>, pg. 408.

veloped mass society in its present form requires a politics of culture, because it is this
cultural domain which is asserting a growing
influence over social consciousness, and consequently masking the economic, political and ethical contradictions of advanced society. Mills'
work played a large role in the American New
Left's understanding of the political role of
contemporary culture.

Mills' general propositions imply a
direct relationship between the development of the
mode of production, particularly the productive
forces, and the structure of individual personality. Mills asserted that the cultural apparatus
demonstrably influences social consciousness and
in particular interprets the meanings and significance of events as well as providing a plethora of
social stereotypes and categories. The individual
shapes his social relationships partially on his
personal expectations, and consequently Mills
implies that the cultural apparatus has a significant effect on the individual's realization of
his instinctual drives. Mills' analysis established an obvious linkage between the economic
dimension of society and individual behavior.

Interpreted from this perspective, Mills'
work paved the road for the popularization of
Marcuse and other "Freudian Marxists." Mills not
only identified the problem of consciousness as
linked to the fragmentation of individual experience, he also outlined the intensified relationship between the cultural domain and the
economic. By implying a political relationship
between the private choices of everyday life and
the public forces of developed industrial society,
Mills' work introduced the question of personality
development into the intellectual framework of the
American Left.

One Dimensionality and the Work of Her-
bert Marcuse

The question of social consciousness and
everyday life is the central focus of Herbert

Marcuse's main writings.[1] His work goes well beyond Mills, extending and refining the politics of culture argument. Marcuse seeks to explain the dialectic of an administered society where the "natural" antagonsims of the capitalist social structure lie dormant. According to Marcuse advanced industrial society is characterized by the absence of the negative impulses of the formerly antagonistic realms, such as labor and capital, replacing them with a single dimension of mutually beneficial and harmonious bureaucratic and technological administration. At least, the appearance of the merger of the formerly hostile realms dominates the empirical world; that is to say, the dominant social consciousness of the mass of persons comprising advanced industrial society does not identify the old antagonistic realms as historically relevant. Marcuse's analysis of one dimensionality outlines the social control of consciousness and the significant changes in the character of the productive forces. In general, his basic assertion is that the new forms of social control and the qualitative changes in the productive forces have not resulted in a new social equilibrium in the amelioration of class conflict but rather these factors have produced a new, qualitative change in the relationship between the productive forces and the relations of production. The consequence of Marcuse's analysis is the assertion of a new dialectic governing this historical period.

> "In this society, the productive apparatus tends to become totalitarian to the extent to which it determines not only the socially needed occupations. skills,

---

[1]This section of this manuscript will treat the following works by Herbert Marcuse: One Dimensional Man (Boston: Beacon Press, 1964); Eros and Civilization (Boston: Beacon, 1956); An Essay on Liberation (Boston: Beacon, 1969); and Counterrevolution and Revolt (Boston: Beacon, 1972).

and attitudes, but also individual needs and aspirations. It thus obliterates the opposition between the private and public existence, between individual and social needs."[1]

Marcuse states that advanced technological and industrial society increases the probability of freedom from material want but it provides this economic security at the cost of a totally administered system. In effect, this system abolishes the categories of social autonomy, critical thought and political opposition. Developed society contains the economic and technological prerequisites for the transendence of material scarcity, but Marcuse is arguing that bureaucratization and social repression accompany the centralized administrative apparatus necessary for the smooth functioning of advanced industrial society. This system, when uninterrupted by political and social antagonisms, produces an ever increasing standard of living and in absolute terms is approaching a post-scarcity capability. The logic of this system is its own defense. Its technological and economic superiority require a centralized decision-making process and the continuous cooperation of its public. Interruption of the system produces less growth, and ultimately, individual unhappiness. Rational thought is system supportive. Rational politics is system supportive. Antagonistic pursuits in either of these realms are irrational by definition. Antagonistic or negative realms are precluded by the logic of the advanced industrial system. In short, Marcuse concludes that the constantly growing standard of living reduces nonconformity in whatever form to "socially useless" activity.

Marcuse describes this system as a totally dominant one. In every sense it obliterates all

---

[1]Marcuse, Introduction, One Dimensional Man, pg. xv.

private experience and any concept of self. "By virtue of the way it has organized its technological base," Marcuse writes, "contemporary industrial society tends to be totalitarian."[1] Marcuse asserts the total domination of all spheres of individual life: in this historical epoch man is confronted with hegemony of this system in all aspects of his life, including the mundane tasks of everyday life. Marcuse implies that commonplace activity is not only political activity, but these everyday activities are so much a reflection of instinctual reflexes that they become critically relevant in a society of manipulated and administered behavior. The domination of advanced industrial society is total. As Marcuse writes:

> "For totalitarian is not only a terroristic political coordination of society, but also a non terroristic economic-technical coordination which operates through the manipulation of needs by vested interests."[2]

The one dimensional society suspends social antagonisms through its ability to create and satisfy "false" needs. Marcuse defines false needs as:

> "those which are superimposed upon the individual by particular social interest, in his repression: the needs which perpetuate toil, aggressiveness, misery and injustice."[3]

Marcuse's analysis is compatible with characterization of the role played by the cultural apparatus. Synthesizing Mills and Marcuse one can argue that the mass society of late capitalism features

---

[1] Ibid., pg. 3.

[2] Ibid., pg. 3.

[3] Ibid., pg. 5.

an ideological sector which obliterates the separation of public and private experience. This is
particularly true with regard to reliance of the
individual on the cultural apparatus for interpretation of the social significance of real life
experiences. Meanwhile this same apparatus pro-
fesses to cherish the value of "individualism" and
promotes a social consciousness which assumes that
the separation of public and private is not only
possible but inevitable. In reality, however,
there is no "private." Contemporary social consciousness is "false" because it assumes there is
a private realm. But there can be no private
realm in a society where the cultural apparatus of
that society maintains the capability to reprogram
the instinctual drives of its citizens such that
false needs are created within the instinctual
makeup of the individual. These "false needs"
maintain the growth and profit of the dominant
vested interests and they are easily satisfied by
them as long as they can be contained within the
commodity form.

Marcuse is asserting that man's instincts are programmed to the interests that
maintain the domination of one dimensionality.
This capability of mass manipulation - or cultural
hegemony - allows for a non-terroristic political
domination by these ruling interests. As long as
false needs can be created by the cultural
apparatus, society can enjoy an unlimited variety
of choices - as long as these choices are
contained within the administered political
borders of the one dimensional society. As
Marcuse writes:

> "The range of choice open to the indi-
> vidual is not the decisive factor in
> determining the degree of human freedom,
> but what can be chosen and what is
> chosen by the individual."[1]

---

[1] Ibid., pg. 7.

The implications of Marcuse's analysis lead to the conclusion that advanced industrial society is a totally reified world, marked by the objectification of interpersonal relationships and characterized by the personal estrangement, as outlined by Marx in The Manuscripts, but now more perniciously orchestrated and so overwhelmingly complete as to threaten an indefinite historical rigidity. Marcuse's analysis forecasts a seemingly impenetrable political universe where the productive forces are capable of a continuously expanding affluence and where the cultural domain is concommitantly capable of "producing" a supportive social consciousness that obliterates the self and former distinctions between self and society, that blends objects and people, and in which society's individuals are libidinously strapped to the administered totality. As Marcuse writes:

> "The people recognize themselves in their commodities: they find their soul in their automobile, hi fi set, split-level home, kitchen equipment. The very mechanism which ties the individual to his society has changed, and social control is anchored in the new needs which it has produced."[1]

In Freudian terms the formerly antagonistic relationship between the pleasure principle and the reality principle is now replaced with the continuous harmony of the two as the cultural apparatus and the sheer domination of the productive forces mold a new pleasure principle, which serves as the synonym for the reality principle. Technological domination through "mass production and mass distribution claim the entire individual."[2]

---

[1] Ibid., pg. 9.

[2] Ibid., pg. 10.

To Marcuse the new epoch, characterized by Daniel Bell as the "end of ideology," in reality is marked not by the absence of ideology but rather by its total domination. Advanced industrial society offers major advances in the material life of the individual, but this progress is a consequence of a highly developed technological base that is ideologically legitimized by its own logic of technological efficiency and productivity. The quality of human activity - real and ideal - is measured against this criterion of efficiency, and consequently all negative forms and thoughts are either coopted by the self-enclosed system or they are identified in advance as self-evidently utopian.

> "Thus emerges a pattern of one-dimensional thought and behavior in which ideas, aspirations, and objectives that, by their content, transcend the established universe of discourse and action are either repelled or reduced to terms of this universe."[1]

The one dimensional society is not without its own dialectical tension, according to Marcuse. The "negation of the negation" is at work within the irrational character of the system's rationality. A system producing the qualitative change envisioned in the promise of advanced technological society concommitantly expands the parameters of human imagination. The one dimensionality of the technological state is transcended by the expectations generated by the more complete conquest of nature and the "ever more effective utilization of its resources." At some point, advanced industrial society is captured by the dialectical tension of its own internal contradiction - the technological possibility of freedom from material scarcity and economic deprivation produced by a cold administrative

---

[1]Ibid., pg. 12.

63

efficiency and a rigid social arrangement that is founded on both the old forms of political repression and the new forms of instinctual manipulation and containment. This universe is contradicted by a new realm of human expectations, flowing from the new possibilities of the productive forces that promises a qualitative historical leap forward where "Life as an end is qualitatively different from life as a means."[1]

To Marcuse the one dimensional society "closes the political universe" because its totalitarian character allows for the absorption of political opposition. It is a society where it appears that class distinctions have given way in the face of the promise of continued upward mobility. It is a society where the state and the corporate sectors have obliterated all but the cosmetic borders that separated them. It is a society where art no longer serves as the REFUSAL of society, or at least represents an ambivalent attitude towards political authority; now art itself becomes part of the one dimensional mass consumption culture.

To Marcuse, labor is no longer the great historical antagonist in the late capitalism of the one dimensional society. Marcuse questions Marx's theorem of the organic composition of capital and his theory of surplus value. Advanced industrial society is an automated society and, according to Marcuse, it is not technology which determines productivity and not the living labor of its present-day workers. Now technology creates the surplus. The automated plant integrates the worker into the technological design of the factory and not vice versa. These are qualitative changes in the character of work, which result in "a weakening of the negative position of the working class: the latter no longer appears

---

[1] Ibid., pg. 17.

64

to be the living contradiction to the established
society."[1]

    The ultimate answer as to whether labor
is the source of wealth or whether its primary
role in the production process is now significantly modified by automation is not critical to
Marcuse's analysis.[1] It will stand regardless of
the resolution of this particular section of his
analysis. What is crucial is that the productive
forces have undergone a qualitative change in that
they are automated to such an advanced degree that
the domination by these forces appears overwhelming. Whether or not the effect of this domination
is a complete conquest of the worker is another
question, that must be assessed in an overall

---

[1]Ibid., pg. 31.

[2]Crucial to Marcuse's argument about the declining
role of the working class in the production of
society's wealth during the period of late capitalism is a long quotation from Marx's Grundrisse.
In Marcuse's version of Marx: "The surplus labor
of the mass has thus caused to be the condition
for the development of social wealth . . .".
Martin Nicolaus offered a different interpretation
almost ten years later in his translation of the
complete edition of the entire work. (K. Marx,
Grundrisse, T.R. M. Nicolaus - [New York: Vintage, 1973]). In his introduction to the translation, Nicolaus denies that Marx's passage can be
interpreted to mean that within the advanced
stages of capitalism, labor will no longer be the
source of surplus and wealth. Nicolaus writes,
"It would ignor Marx's unambiguous statements, in
many other passes, that there are counter-tenden-
cies which prevent mechanization and automation
from advancing beyond a certain limited point,
under capitalism; such a counter-tendency, for
example is the decline of the rate of
profit . . .".

critique of Marcuse's concept of one dimensionality. (See last chapter on mimetic versus one
dimensaional praxis).

Marcuse's one dimensionality connotes an
ideological domination over the processes that
develop social consciousness. A part of that
process has been what Marcuse refers to as high
culture - art, culture, religion, literature, etc.
Within mass consumption and the mass production
ethic of late capitalism, high culture, which was
previously antagonistic or ambivalent about social
authority, is now "transformed into popular culture." To Marcuse high culture served as the
provider of a range of sublimated images and
future visions of the human imagination, which
allowed negations of the present order to be
fashioned surreptiously in this elite realm of
society. However, according to Marcuse advanced
capitalism allows for the desublimation of these
images because they can become coopted by the
system when they are popularized within the exchange ethic and the commodity form. Advanced
industrial society is characterized by this desublimation of previously taboo images and actions,
but it is also marked by the repressive social
framework which contains them, giving rise to a
"repressive desublimation." It is this repressive
desublimation - the popularization and "sale" of
previously antagonistic ideas and actions - which
provides the basic aspect of social control within
Marcuse's conceptualization of the one dimensional
society; this phenomenom of repressive desublimation allows for late capitalism to contain its
contradictions through the pacification of the
mass by absorbing subversive social elements.
Repressive desublimation in the one dimensional
society ensures the safety of the political status
quo, because all forms of opposition to the existing social order can now be contained even in
their enjoyed popularity; their subversive character is negated by the system-supportive influence
of the cultural apparatus that possesses the
capability of reprogramming the basic instinctual
drives of the individual and guaranteeing a libidinal bond to the political order. Marcuse's

66

characterization of the one dimensional society leads him to the conclusion that the political universe is closed.

The concept of repressive desublimation is founded on Marcuse's synthesis of Freudian psychology and Marx's socio-economic categories. Freud outlines his social psychological analysis in Civilization and its Discontents[1] and Marcuse relies primarily on that work in his freudian marxian synthesis, which he presents in Eros and Civilization.

Freud wrote that civilization is founded on the individual's sublimation of his instinctual pleasure drives. Man is biologically inclined to pursue all feelings of pleasure and avoid episodes involving displeasure. As Freud wrote:

". . . our normal mental life exhibits oscillations between a comparatively easy liberation of pleasure and a comparatively difficult one, parallel with which there goes a diminished or an increased receptivity to unpleasure."[2]

Man soon learns that there are forces external to his own being which can bring both pleasure and unhappiness. Man can significantly influence these experiences by his own activities and choices. The reality of the external world conflicts with the pleasure of sensual gratification brought by the pursuit of the individual's instinctual drives. In short, Freud outlines two main principles that surround human experience, the reality and pleasure principles.

Civilization is an attempt to enlist the human will in the struggle for the domination over

---

[1]Sigmund Freud, Civilization and Its Discontents (New York: W. W. Norton & Company, 1962).

[2]Ibid., pg. 25.

the external calamities and potential harms of nature. This subjugation of nature to man - that is the birth of civilization - requires uniformity and order. The required predictability and order necessary for civilization imposes a cost on the individual, the modification of the instinctual drives. In short, Freud asserts that civilization requires the conquest of the pleasure princple by the reality principle. This is the sublimation of instincts, in which:

> "One may therefore hope to be freed from a part of one's suffering by influencing the instinctual impulses. This type of defence against suffering is no longer brought to bear on the sensory apparatus; it seeks to master the internal sources of our needs."[1]

Civilization is the source of repression. The uniformity, conformity and submission necessary for civilization preclude the free exercise of the instinctual impulses because their unbounded liberation is subversive to the prerequisites of order and regimentation. The instincts of sexual pleasure and aggression, for instance, are disintegrating elements.

Civilization is the source of neurosis. The individual who is unable to modify his impulses will not find happiness. As Freud wrote:

> "Happiness, in the reduced sense in which we recognize it as possible, is a problem of the economics of the individual's libido."[2]

Those who mismanage this "economy" are bound for

---

[1] Ibid., pg. 26.

[2] Ibid., pg. 30.

emotional instability. Man benefits from the security (Anacke) offered by the order brought by civilization at the cost of yielding or modifying his instincts (Eros) and the emotional oscillations resulting from the administration of the reality principle's domination of the pleasure principle are reflections of the ebbs and flows of this inevitable neurotic affliction.

Freud developed the concept of "superego" in explaining the complicated regulatory process that maintains the necessary levels of instinctual sublimation and the superiority of the reality principle. In studying primitive society, Freud argued that the creation of taboos and totems were crucial for the maintenance of these civilizations.[1] The taboo became a regulator of human conduct, developed in order to establish certain societal relationships and avoid others. Although violation of a taboo would be met with physical punishment, Freud wrote that:

> "Taboo is a command of conscience, the violation of which causes a terrible sense of guilt which is as self-evident as its origin is unknown."[2]

To Freud the phenomenon of conscience as self regulator of the instinctual impulses was not unique to primitive populations but rather conscience and guilt were characteristic of all civilizations. Within each individual, his ego (conscious) is confronted by the super ego:

> ". . . which now, in the form of 'conscience,' is ready to put into action against the ego the same harsh aggressiveness that the ego would have liked to satisfy upon other, extraneous indi-

---

[1] Sigmund Freud, Totem and Taboo (New York: Vintage Books, 1946).

[2] Ibid., pg. 90.

viduals. The tension between the harsh
super-ego and the ego that is subjected
to it, is called by us the sense of
guilt."[1]

It is conscience and guilt which regulate the antagonism between the reality and pleasure principles, maintaining the former's superiority.

The individual's fear of the loss of
social acceptance gives rise to a sense of guilt
that is realized in the internalization of this
fear. The anxiety generated by the fear of the
disobedience of external authority plays on the
conscience of the individual and results in his
yielding to his feelings of guilt.

"First comes renunciation of instinct
owing to fear of aggression by the external authority . . . After that comes
the erection of an internal authority,
and renunciation of instinct owing to
Fear of it - owing to fear of conscience."[2]

According to Freud, civilization by its
very nature results in the self-estrangement of
the individual due to the necessity of self-
repression expressed in the form of guilt. Social
order is dependent on this self-regulatory process
within the individual. However, Marcuse's description of advanced industrial society as one
dimensional identifies a qualitative change in the
nature of social control. This change in social
hegemony allows for the phenomenon of what Marcuse
terms "repressive desublimation," which qualitatively alters the forms of repression. Whereas
earlier stages of industrial society necessitated
the sublimation of some of the individual's in-

---

[1] Sigmund Freud, Civilization and Its Discontents,
pg. 70.

[2] Ibid., pg. 75.

stinctual drives, advanced industrial society permits the desublimation of these particular instincts because they will be expressed through specific forms which are compatible with the dynamics of modern society. Advanced industrial society is so totally dominant of the cultural development of the individual that the level of taboo that pertained under the less developed industrial form can now be represented as historically obsolete due to the post scarcity capability of the modern productive forces.

> "Freed from the sublimated form which was the very token of its irreconcilable dreams - a form which is the style, the language in which the story is told - sexuality turns into a vehicle for the bestsellers of oppression. It could not be said of any of the sexy women in contemporary literature what Balzac says of the whore Esther: that hers was the tenderness which blossoms only in infinity. This society turns everything it touches into a potential source of progress and of exploitation, of drudgery and satisfaction, of freedom and of oppression. Sexuality is no exception."[1]

Marcuse attempts to synthesize Freud and Marx by integrating Marx's historical specificity with Freud's psycho-social analysis. Marcuse wants to interrelate ideology and the structure of personality with the mode of production. He thus replaces Freud's a-historical reality principle with his "performance principle." The performance principle is "the prevailing historical form of the reality principle."[2] Accounting for Marx's historical understanding of the development of political economy, Marcuse states that different

---

[1] Marcuse, op cit., pgs. 77-78.

[2] Herbert Marcuse, Eros and Civilization, pg. 35.

civilizations may produce different reality principles. He writes, "The various modes of domination (of men and nature) result in various historical forms of the reality principle."[1] As the modes of domination vary, so too does the level of repression such that maintenance of a class structured society demands an external level of repression beyond that necessary for the maintenance of civilization. "These additional controls arising from the specific institutions of domination are what we denote as surplus repression."[2] In a world free from material scarcity, Marcuse states that the possibility of "non-repressive" sublimation may be realized and surplus repression would cease to exist as a characteristic of social order.

Advanced industrial society retains a surplus repression beyond the amount of sublimation required for the maintenance of civilization. Within the context of Marcuse's one dimensional society, the phenomenon of repressive desublimation allows for the containment of previously taboo images and activities within the commodity form and within a general societal framework which accomplishes the reprogramming of the instinctual drives for their harmonious juncture with the modern performance principle. As Marcuse writes:

> ". . . it is desublimation practiced from a 'position of strength' on the part of society, which can afford to grant more than before because its interests have become the inner-most drives of its citizens, and because the joys which it grants promote social cohesion and contentment."[3]

---

[1] Ibid., pg. 37.

[2] Ibid., pg. 37.

[3] Marcuse, One Dimensional Man, pg. 72.

In short, the pleasure and performance (reality) principles merge in the one dimensional society, maintaining a system of total domination. Marcuse concludes that no longer must a repressive reprogramming of the instincts be accomplished; the instinctual drives are granted within this mode of domination.

Within this repressed desublimation and reconciliation of the pleasure and reality principles, the realization of pleasure generates submission. A "happy consciousness" replaces the regulatory function of the conscience, for now the very indulgence by the manipulated society. Consequently, false consciousness becomes true consciousness and all antagonisms are absorbed. "Conscience is absolved by reification, by the general necessity of things."[1] The subjective forces are absorbed by the structure of advanced industrial society.

Marcuse and the New Praxis

The pessimism expressed in One Dimensional Man is significantly modified in Marcuse's later writing, which responds to the emergence of the New Left. In An Essay on Liberation and also in Counterrevolution and Revolt, Marcuse outlines the nature of the central contradiction at work within the one dimensional society and postulates that a new praxis will forge the qualitative breakthroughs in social consciousness necessary to negate the one dimensionality of advanced industrial society.

However, for the realization of these new possibilities presented by material promise of advanced society, Marcuse writes that a new human "sensibility" must emerge. It is the development of the post scarcity potential of the modern forces which promises a qualitative leap in the relations of production when accompanied by new

---

[1]Ibid., pg. 79.

forms of organization and ultimately a concommitant change in social consciousness.

> ". . . the development of the productive forces beyond their capitalist organization suggests the possibility of freedom <u>within</u> the realm of necessity."[1]

Only a revolution and a revolutionary praxis can "rupture" the closed universe of the one dimensional society.

> "The new sensibility has become by this very token <u>praxis</u>: it emerges in the struggle against violence and exploitation where this struggle is waged for essentially new ways and forms of life: negation of the entire Establishment, its morality, culture . . .".[2]

The implication of Marcuse's analysis is that any revolution against a society that has libidinally captured its citizens must encounter the one dimensional society within the private everyday realm - the structure of personality itself - as well as the more public arenas of the superstructure and the base. He stresses that a system that finds its political strength within the "biological" makeup of the individual can be defeated only by waging a struggle over the control of the new politicized libido. A revolutionary praxis for advanced industrial society must necessarily assert a politics of the personal. Marcuse's view is quite different from C. Wright Mills, who expressed this quite differently when he referred to the necessity of the "sociological imagination" to clarify the public (political) nature of the private - history and biography - and for the translation of this new consiousness into social action. In synthesizing both Mills and Marcuse

---

[1] Marcuse, <u>An Essay on Liberation</u>, pg. 21.

[2] <u>Ibid</u>., pg. 25.

their respective analyses jointly focus on the cultural dimension of social reality as the dominating force in the foundation of advanced capitalism which leads to its political and economic stability. It is this emphasis on the political role of modern culture which was the unique characteristic of the New Left in theory and practice.

Marcuse asserts that the "progress" of late capitalism is accomplished at the cost of creating unsatisfiable needs, and the inability of modern capitalism to meet these needs becomes its central contradiction. It creates and heightens needs it can never satisfy.

> "The unifying force remains a force of disintegration. The total organization of society under monopoly capital and the growing wealth created by this organization can neither undo nor arrest the dynamic of its growth: capitalism cannot satisfy the needs which it creates . . . it is now fostering tran-scending needs which cannot be satisfied without abolishing the capitalist mode of production . . .".[1]

Revolutionary praxis will involve not an extension of these needs or a reordering of them, but rather a "qualitative leap" which:

> "involves a radical transformation of the needs and aspiration themselves, cultural as well as material; of consciousness and sensibility; of the work process as well as leisure."[2]

Marcuse calls for a new praxis which will include a cultural dimension that openly engages the

---

[1]Herbert Marcuse, Counterrevolution and Revolt, pg. 16.

[2]Ibid., pgs. 16-17.

75

ideological hegemony represented in the everyday world of the reified society. To Marcuse the new praxis must engage all the fundamental values that maintain the commodity form in all of its systemic realms - economic, political, social, and psychological. Within the context of the one dimensional hegemony of monopoly capitalism and by its absorption of the previously antagonistic forces, revolutionary change requires changes within the need structure of the working class itself because according to Marcuse the working class remains the central agency for political change in an advanced society. Since in theory no other force within society possesses the political potential of this class, Marcuse asserts that it can be the only revolutionary subject within this historical age.

"The latter [monopoly capitalism] can be brought down only by those who will sustain the established work process, who constitute its human base, who reproduce its profits and power."[1]

This agency can only realize itself with the birth of a new consciousness and a new praxis that breaks the hegemonic control and the libidinal domination of the modern personality. To Marcuse the new praxis must politically recapture the private realm from the political onslaught of the cultural apparatus and the commodity form.

Marcuse admits the absence of a working class culture and consciousness. Since it has been dispossessed from the previously private realms of consciousness and consequently denied any concept of "self," this class has been subsumed by its masters. To Marcuse the "biological" domination of the modern working class has left them without a world. To Marcuse its consciousness lives on the meager fringes of the ruling class consciousness, hoping that simple ideological replication will bring upward mobility or at

---

[1]Ibid., pg. 132.

least maintain its middle level hierarchial privilege. Marcuse's understanding of working class culture and consciusness is simply that it does not exist. It was obliterated in the ravenous assault on the "private" during monopoly capitalism's conquest of the personality.

Marcuse asserts that only a revolutionary praxis will forge a new sensibility and reawaken the now dormant Revolutionary Subject. The new praxis must center itself on the juncture between the socio-economic realm of the "public" and the psychological arena of the instinctual and the "private." Any praxis which denies this focus will, at best, result in changes in form but not substance. As Bruce Brown writes:

> "Revolutionary praxis in the one dimensional society must contend with a dynamic comprehension of the factors underlying everyday life and the forces conditioning the psychic development of the individual personality."[1]

As stated below (Part II) New Left practice became the opposite of revolutionary practice by sliding back into either the Old Left puritanism or the anarcho-cultural evasion of the dominant social praxis.

Utopianism and Marcuse's One Dimensionality

Although I will reserve the final chapter of this manuscript for a thorough criticism of the New Left Idea and assessment of its relationship to the American Student Movement, it is important to note here some general criticisms of Marcuse's arguement. In brief they revolve around his economic analysis and what is alleged to be his non-dialectical and a-historical argument.

---

[1]Bruce Brown, *Marx, Freud and the Critique of Everyday Life* (New York: Monthly Review Press, 1973), pg. 22.

The general criticism concerning the utopian character of Marcuse's work usually focuses on his vision of the new society.[1] Peter Clecak's Radical Paradoxes asserts that Marcuse's concept of man is unrealistic and that overall his analysis is more myth than reality.

"Marcuse finally produces a kind of fiction that he represents as social theory. The implicit fictional form ironically parallels the disastrous confusion of social theory and aesthetics that his postwar essays often exhibit."[2]

Although Clecak refuses to confront Marcuse's analysis of culture and the development of contemporary social consciousness, he does not hesitate to criticize the more eschatological aspects of Marcuse's future society. The thrust of Clecak's charge of utopianism may stand, without, however, affecting Marcuse's general analysis. However, if Marcuse's work has any intellectual merit, it rests with his attempt to discover the reasons for the failure of a viable American socialist movement and his contribution is his influence on the

---

[1] Among a variety of works, particularly see: Jack Woodis, New Theories of Revolution (New York: International Publishers, 1972); Peter Clecak, Radical Paradoxes, op cit.; George Litchtheim, "From Marx to Hegel: Reflections on George Lukacs, T. W. Adorno, and Herbert Marcuse," Triquarterly No. 12, Spring 1968. The utopian character of Marcuse's work is criticized by all of the above but Martin Jay expressed it as, ". . . there is no necessary reason to suppose that a new society, however rational, would satisfy all of men's needs or end all his fears. Above all, the mystery of death and the arbitrariness of suffering would make human existence a continuing subject for the aesthetic imagination."

[2] Clecak, op cit., pgs. 228-229.

"cultural" direction of contemporary social
theory. To Marcuse failure is rooted in the
libidinal perversion of the personality by the
technological rationality of late capitalism.
Thus the assessment of social consciousness and
its related processes as it appears in Marcuse's
work, is the initial step in any attempt in surveying the prospects for various modes of socialism around the world. As a student of Marcuse,
Jeremy Shapiro, has written:

> ". . . if critical consciousness is a
> prerequisite of revolution, then we must
> take seriously the nature of the con-
> sciousness that preceeds it if we are to
> understand the transition from one to
> another. Hence we must recognize the
> constitutive importance of legitimiza-
> tion (mythical and ideological) in the
> social order."[1]

The more persuasive and critical assessments of Marcuse's one dimensionality focus on the
assumptions and assertions involving political
economy. The major revision of Marx's theory
contained in One Dimensional Man is Marcuse's
dismissal of the traditional theory of surplus
value and the organic composition of capital.
Essentially Marcuse is asserting that a surplus
product emanates from technology itself; consequently labor becomes a diminishing and ultimately
nonexistent source of wealth.[2]

In orthodox-marxist critique of Marcuse's political economy, Paul Mattick attacks
Marcuse for assuming constantly increasing production and productivity resulting in an ever-

---

[1]Jeremy Shapiro, "The Dialectic of Theory and
Practice in the Age of Technological Rationality:
Herbert Marcuse and Jurgen Habermas," in D. Howard
and K. Klare, op cit.., pg. 289.

[2]Marcuse, One Dimensional Man, pgs. 27-28.

rising standard of living.[1] Mattick argues that it is not production and productivity which are the driving forces behind capitalism but rather surplus and profit which result in capital. Increases in wasteful production will not yield new capital, therefore not all growth contributes to the capital stock. Government induced production is not always capital yielding, as in the case of military production. Marcuse's assertion about the continued increase in the overall stock of production without an explanation of what kind of production and under what conditions leaves his analysis with less than a satisfactory explanation of a major factor in his argument. Further, Marcuse assumes that modern capitalism is dominated by technology rather than vice versa.

Marcuse asserts that as automation and advanced technology reduce the necessary labor time in the production process, labor ceases to be the source of wealth. As previously noted (pg. 65, footnote 2), Marcuse cites the Grundrisse in order to bolster his point. Mattick, however, argues, "Where there is no labour, there can be no surplus-labour and consequently, no accumulation of capital."[2] Any other source of capital fundamentally alters the character of capitalism and suggests the emergence of a new mode of production. Mattick writes, ". . . that a reduction in labor-time which would disturb the necessary relationship between surplus-value and capital is not compatible with capitalism and will, for that reason, interrupt, or end, the capitalist production process."[3]

---

[1] Paul Mattick, Critique of Marcuse: One Dimensional Man in Class Society (New York: Herder and Herder, 1972).

[2] Ibid., pg. 29.

[3] Ibid., pg. 30.

Mattick identifies the fundamental problem with maintaining the marxist character of Marcuse's political economy in One Dimensional Man. Capitalism cannot allow the totally automated economy to surface or even approach realization for it will result either in a critical crisis of disproportionality where the consequent over-production will harden disaster or it will identify a new mode of production and the death of capitalism by Marx's definition.

> "What Marcuse considers a capitalistic solution to capitalism's difficulties, namely, its new technology, represents, instead, the present and future insoluble contradiction of capital production within property relations of the market economy."[1]

Mattick's view of Marx's statement about automation in the Grundrisse as 'labor ceasing to be the source of wealth' is really Marx's reference to a post-capitalist world where "the abolition of value realtions is the abolition of capitalism itself."[2]

The utopianism of Marcuse and the weakness of his political economy do not critically damage his analysis of contemporary social consciousness under late capitalism because the critical commentary strikes at the optimistic character concerning the possibilities for future man under a new society. However, serious challenges can be made with regard to the one dimensional description of contemporary social consciousness and, in general, his interpretation of cultural hegemony and everyday life [see last chapter].

---

[1] Ibid., pg. 42.

[2] Ibid., pg. 47.

Summary

The critique of cultural hegemony and everyday life was the foundation of the New Left Idea. The major aspect of New Left intellectual thought was its examination of the relationship between political economy and the structure of personality. C. Wright Mills initially identified the focus of the New Left Idea as the juncture between public issues and private troubles. Marcuse began with a similar starting point but placed his explanation in the categories of his freudian-marxist synthesis. Marcuse moved the New Left Idea to its central concern with the processes developing social consciousness. The New Left sought an assessment of contemporary consciousness and its radical potential. The New Left Idea concentrated on the relationship between the cultural dimension, the development of personality and everyday life behavior in order to explain the broader connection between the socioeconomic structure and social consciousness.

The traditional marxism of the Old Left failed to investigate the political context of the cultural apparatus except in very broad and deterministic terms. The Old Left approached the question of false consciousness with sole reference to its determined character governed by the status of the productive forces. To the Old Left the inevitable breakdown of capitalism's internal mechanism would rectify the false nature of the contemporary consciousness. Little, if any, attempt was made to reconcile the social prerequisites of attitudes, values, cultures that precondition political movements and their distinct national characters. With the prolonged strength of the capitalist system amply demonstrated in the West by the late fifties, the New Left Idea and its freudian-marxist predecessors surfaced with the intellectual vigor, vitality and imagination appropriate for a generation of disillusioned but passionate Americans. To them the New Left Idea and its critique of cultural hegemony and everyday life would be translated into a political practice fashioned around the slogan, "the personal is the political."

82

The cultural hegemony analysis represents a critical breakthrough for the development of an American Marxism. Previous to the New Left, only the Leninist and Social Democratic forms of socialist praxis were historically significant in the United States. The New Left Idea allowed for the general reassessment of these "old" models and attempted to put forth a new praxis rooted in a very different understanding of contemporary social consciousness and focused on the junction between public issues and private orbits.

The New Left Idea was only partially comprised of the cultural hegemony concept. In full, it demands the synthesis of this analysis with the New Left's understanding of advanced capitalism and the question of social agency for change.

The New Left's attempted revisions of
Marx's political economy was its greatest intellectual challenge. The Old Left had reduced its
economic analysis to mechanical prognostications
concerning the inevitable collapse of the modern
capitalist order. The inherent contradictions
contained within the essential irrationality of an
unplanned economy and the illogical thrust towards
the monopolization of industry spelled the un-
avoidable economic catastrophe that would lead to
a massive breakthrough in consciousness and political movement. To the Old Left, economic theory
became the constant search for the telltale indi-
cations of economic downturn. All indices supporting the sound economic health of modern capitalism were reinterpreted to suggest their support
for arguments hypothesizing the exact opposite
condition. Marx demonstrated the impenetrable
logic identifying the dialectical collision between the forces of production and the relations
of production. However, the Old Left economic
analysis expected this historical breakthrough as
a cumulative disintegration composed of successive
breakdowns in the normal cyclical pattern of the
capitalist system. The recurring recessions and
depressions were brought on by the system's tendency towards overproduction and underconsumption.
Inevitably the soaring unemployment levels and
general pauperization of society would peak during
one extended economic catastrophe and at some
point this would result in a societal demand for a
new order. Marxist political economy was reduced
to social astronomy. The New Left's attempt to
revive the dynamic quality of marxist political
economy was clearly unsatisfactory, but it did
reopen this dimension of marxist thought.

No definitive New Left political economy has
emerged; the New Left Idea represented an amalgam
of partial revisions of the Old Left interpretation of Marx's model; no one total revision has
taken hold. There was no universally accepted New

Left political economy, but there was a growing literature which sought a comprehensive critique of modern capitalism.[1]

In particular the New Left Idea was concerned with three separate characteristics of late capitalism. These are (1) the theory of the rising surplus and the monopoly economy as identified by Baran and Sweezy in Monopoly Capital; (2) the expanded role of the state in the socialization of costs and the maintenance of foreign outlets for the rising surplus; and (3) the characterization of American capitalism as a "post scarcity" and "post accumulation" system.

The New Left Idea is characterized by its general description of the corporate nature of the state.[2] United States capitalism harbors a growing symbiosis between the executive and bureaucratic realms of the public sector and the near-monopoly dominated industries of the private sector. The corporate state is achieved by the massive consolidation of public and private power for the general benefit of specific vested in-

---

[1]Several works are of significance: Howard Sherman, Radical Political Economy (New York: Basic Books, 1972); James O'Connor, The Fiscal Crisis of the State (New York: St. Martin's Press, 1973); Maurice Godelier, Rationality and Irrationality in Economics (New York: Monthly Review Press, 1973). In addition, the New Left's economic analysis was significantly influenced by Paul Baran and Paul Sweezy, Monopoly Capital (New York: Montly Review Press, 1966).

[2]Although this analysis is presented in a variety of papers, articles and books, the most direct description of the Corporate State position was presented by Daniel Fusfeld, "The Rise of the Corporate State," Journal of Economic Issues, Vol. 1, No. 1, March, 1972, I will use some of Fusfeld's analysis in my brief overview of this general argument.

terests. According to Daniel Fusfeld this new corporate state is a result of three long-term trends in late capitalism: the emergence of the "super" corporation, the rise of a massive state apparatus, and the advent of the multinational corporation.[1]

The super corporation is marked by an authoritarian and heirarchial internal structure. The main political body within the organization is the management and not outside stockholders. Management becomes "self selecting," while obviously retaining the feature of a private government whose decisions on product, prices, investments and employment levels affect the entire social fabric.

The rise of what Fusfeld entitles "the positive state" accompanies the severe concentration in corporate power that distinguishes late capitalism from its previous form. The growth in the number of governmental agencies and the overall monetary size of Federal expenditures imply the increase in economic influence that has accrued to the state sector. The thrust of this apparatus is (1) the universal distribution of the costs of technological innovation, which increases productivity and lowers unit costs; (2) the direct and indirect subsidization of profit; (3) the legitimization of the present configuration of power via a variety of social expenses, and (4) the pursuit of a vigorous foreign policy that allows for the continued presence of American capital around the world.

The development of the multinational corporation and the general penetration of the major world markets by American capital have been dependent on the growing alliance between the private and public sectors. The extensive reach of American capital requires a state recognition

---

[1] Ibid.

of the imperative and fragile nature of all political and economic activity in present and future markets. The scope of American imperialism is considerably widened and it requires the services of an extensive foreign policy marked by its acute awareness of the delicate interdependencies involved within international events. The near merger of the public and private sectors is the definitive characteristic of late capitalism. According to Birnbaum:

> "The intervention of the state in the sphere of production is so very great as to make dubious the very term intervention."[1]

To Birnbaum the role of the public sector is the "control of the level of social investment" and the "provision of an infra-structure without which capitalist accumulation could not continue.[2] The specific features of this new infrastructure are varied in nature but Ernest Mandel has described the most obvious and important.[3] He lists the state's role in the underwriting of technological innovation, the maintenance of a sizeable arms industry, the growth of welfare expenditures to "amortize" economic crises, the introduction and growth of economic planning, and finally the general underwriting of private profit through the socialization of costs. The state plays a critical role in ameliorating the periodic crises of disproportionality, particularly in the charged

---

[1] Norman Birnbaum, "Late Capitalism in the United States" in George Fisher, Revival of American Socialism, op cit., pg. 146.

[2] Ibid., pgs. 145-164.

[3] See Ernest Mandel, Marxist Economic Theory (New York: Monthly Review Press, 1968); also a briefer explanation of Mandel's "neo-capitalism" is contained in: Ernest Mandel, An Introduction to Marxist Economic Theory (New York: Pathfinder Press, 1970).

environment of severe interdependents characteristic of monopoly capitalism.

Under modern capitalism the state is not
perceived as the simple protector of the existing
property relations, but rather it is required to
subsidize capital accumulation through fiscal and
monetary policy as well as intervening in capital's struggle to contain labor and maintian the
present relations of production. This "activist"
role for executive action and federal behavior is
usually associated with "liberal" ideology. The
New Left and the American Student Movement identified the corporate bias of the liberal ideal by
outlining the corporate beneficiaries of liberal
government. In so doing, the New Left referred to
modern capitalism as "corporate liberalism."
Corporate liberalism, then, reflects the revision-
ist character of modern capitalism in the United
States, including its imperialist instincts. The
roots of this corporate liberalism lie partly in
its ideological and cultural hegemony and partly
in its monopoly and bureaucratic features. Its
capability for continuous growth and expansion is
in part based on its ability in shaping mass distribution and consumption, a direct function of
the cultural realm of everyday life. Its economic
growth is also dependent on the continuous presence of the factors of mass production which is a
direct function of its monopolistic and bureaucratic concentrations of political and economic
power. The term "corporate liberalism" identifies
the ideological and also the economic nature of
late capitalism.

Monopoly Capital and the Rising Surplus

As previously stated, Marx's theory of
crisis holds that the periodic disruptions cyclic-
ly experienced by the capitalist system were a
direct function of the system's tendency towards
overproduction. As the growth of the productive
forces was generated by previous investment provided by the system's overall surplus, this growth
eventually stimulated new sources of investment.
However, at some regular interval, the amount of

investment exceeded that which the system was capable of absorbing. An upward limit on production was reached and surpassed whereby overall production outstrips consumption. Inventories swell. Production is reduced and with it unemployment rises. Consumption falls until is proportion to investment increased to the point that investment is renewed and the cycle is reversed.

Capitalism is plagued by this disproportionality between investment and consumption, rendered more abstractly in marxist theory as the contradiction between the forces and the relations of production. Capitalism suffers from its constant tendency to fail to consume all its produces. The system ends up destroying excess capital instead of utilizing it in rationally addressing human needs. To paraphrase Marx, 'the real enemy of capitalism is capitalism itself.'

Characterized in part by the oligopolistic features of its market structure and the increased role of the state apparatus in the overall activity of the system, modern capitalism is quite different from its earlier design. The emergence of super corporations has been accompanied by monopolization -- or oligopolization -- of the significant industries in the contemporary U.S. economy. Oligopolies pursue many market patterns similar to monopolies but with some major exceptions, most notably the presence of some competing firms. However, oligopolies are characterized by ". . . a systematic avoidance of risk taking and . . . an attitude of live-and-let-live toward other members of the corporate world.[1] These new attitudes represent qualitative changes from the entrepreneur pictured in the "laissez-faire" epoch of capitalist development.

The hierarchical and bureaucratic organization of the giant corporation in the oligopolistic industry allows for risks to be more

---

[1] Baran & Sweezy, op cit., pg. 48.

89

carefully calculated. The absence of numerous competitors and the mass consumption process provide an easier area to survey and assess short- and long-term trends. In the highly concentrated industry, giant corporations can avoid mutually destructive relationships while maintaining a "competitive" corporate structure.

According to Baran and Sweezy the super corporation attempts to avoid price decreases brought on by industry competition and replaces prices with other less destructive methods of corporate competition. Price cuts by one industrial firm will not necessarily result in its extending its share of the market but rather most likely results in all firms' lowering their respective prices in similar proportion and all firms within the industry will have suffered. In the world of monopoly capital, price competition is acknowledged as mutually destructive behavior.

"To void such situations, therefore, becomes the first concern of corporate policy, the 'sine qua non' of orderly and profitable business operation . . . This objective is achieved by the simple expedient of banning price cutting as a legitimate weapon of economic warfare."[1]

The oligopolies of monopoly capitalism similarly seek to maximize their profits, and as did the previous entrepreneurs of early capitalism, expand their share of the industry's market. However, the dramatic reduction in the number of corporate actors in the respective industries has highlighted the severe degree of interdependence which binds the super corporations to one another. Price competition is a "no win" game in which the consumer is the only beneficiary. Administered prices replace competitive prices, attained through direct collusion or through disguised and indirect forms of communication about a firm's

---

[1] *Ibid.*, pg. 58.

respective price behavior. In the view of Baran and Sweezy:

> "The end of the shakedown period naturally does not mean the end of the struggle for larger market shares; it simply means the end of price competition as a weapon in that struggle. The struggle itself goes on, but with other weapons."[1]

Under monopoly capitalism, the elimination of price competition intensifies the corporate pressure for cost decreases. The low cost, high profit oligopolist usually maintains a superior position within its respective industry.

> "The firm with the lowest costs holds the whip hand; it can afford to be aggressive even to the point of threatening, and in the limiting case precipitating a price war."[2]

The low cost firm enjoys a variety of advantages over its competitors:

> "It can afford the advertising, research, development of new product varieties, extra services, and so on, which are the usual means of fighting for market shares. . .".[3]

In addition the low cost firm establishes a strong reputation with its customers, potential employees, officers and related professional ranks.

The operations of an oligopolistic economy and its accompanying cost-cutting prac-

---

[1] Ibid., pg. 64.

[2] Ibid., pgs. 68-69.

[3] Ibid., pg. 69.

tices have significant implications for orthodox marxist theory. As Baran and Sweezy stated:

> "It is true, as we have argued that oligopolies succeed in attaining a close approximation to the theoretical monopoly price and if their never-ceasing efforts to cut costs . . . are generally successful, then it follow with inescapable logic that surplus must have a strong and persistent tendency to rise."[1]

Baran and Sweezy counterpose their law of rising surplus to Marx's theorem of the falling rate of profit. They revise Marx's theorem because ". . . the structure of the capitalist economy has undergone a fundamental change . . .".[2] Capitalism has passed from its competitive stage to a new monopoly stage where the competitive market and its accentuation on price competition have been replaced by cost cutting and a general oligopolistic market structure.

The tendency for rising surplus marks the new historical epoch of capitalist development, monopoly capitalism. This new stage is characterized by the giant corporation, the oligopolistic market structure and the new forms of market competition, which most notably include the sales effort and the entire spectrum of ideological support generated by the cultural apparatus. The latter aids in the oligopolists' concentration on product development and mass manipulation which justify the trend of every-increasing administered prices.

The fundamental tasks facing monopoly capitalism -- or corporate liberalism -- is the absorption of the ever-increasing surplus. Baran

---

[1] *Ibid.*, pg. 67.

[2] *Ibid.*, pg. 72.

and Sweezy outline ways in which the surplus is absorbed: consumption, investment, and waste. However, the monopoly capitalist system cannot generate the necessary consumption and investment levels for total absorption, and consequently the system is constantly plagued by a tendency toward fundamental crisis. As Baran and Sweezy stated:

"It tends to generate even more surplus, yet it fails to provide the consumption and investment outlets required for the absorption of a rising surplus and hence the smooth working of the system. Since surplus which cannot be absorbed will not be produced, it follows that the 'normal' state of the monopoly capitalist economy is stagnation."[1]

The three counteracting forces at work in the monopoly capitalist structure are: the sales effort, civilian government, and the expansion of foreign markets through militarism and imperialism. Each of these new or exogenous forces is aimed at ameliorating the crisis of disproportionality by stimulating consumption. The non-competitive system requires these outside forces to increase demand proportionate to the level of overproduction.

The sales effort takes the form of reliance on advertising for the creation of artificial needs to stimulate consumption. Baran's and Sweezy's argumentation here is similar to the point made in the pervious section on "one dimensionality and the critique of everyday life":

". . . the economic importance of advertising lies not primarily in its causing a reallocation of consumers' expenditures among different commodities but in

---

[1]Ibid., pg. 108.

93

its effect on the magnitude of aggregate demand and thus on the level of income and employment."[1]

From this perspective one can begin to synthesize the cultural and economic analyses of the New Left. The functon of cultural hegemony is not simply an ideological matter; the relationship between cultural hegemony and economic stability is crucial. The mass manipulation by the cultural apparatus is primarily concerned with the stimulation of an individual corporate profit margin. In general, the cultural dimension is focused on the expansion of the productive forces through the "proliferation of things" characteristic of monopoly capital and its mass consumption milieux. The integration of Mills, Marcuse and the radical economic critiques of the New Left and its forerunners allows one to understand the context in which social consciousness is significantly shaped. The cultural apparatus, thus, plays a doubly important role -- it is at once the key stimulant in the expansion of consumption and absorption of the surplus product and the creator of a compatible social consciousness.

The economic function of the cultural apparatus is served by the sales effort.

"Price competition has largely receded as a means of attracting the public's custom, and has yielded to new ways of sales promotion: advertising, variation of the products' appearance and packaging, 'planned obsolescence,' model changes, credit schemes, and the like."[2]

The convergence of these respective cultural and economic analyses allows us to clarify the emerg-

---

[1] Ibid., pg. 124.

[2] Ibid., pg. 115.

ing New Left definition of cultural hegemony under advanced capitalism. The product is made more attractive because the cultural apparatus attempts to bestow on it attributes beyond the scope of simple objects. The product is given a personality, characterized by one or more virtues desirable to a conditioned audience that has been culturally denied a "self." The product is possessed by its unusual erotic qualities, or it is characterized by its sheer power in the domination of antagonists, or one of an untold number of other possibilities. In short, monopoly capitalism has fashioned a cultural domain whereby the process of the inversion of consciousness has come full circle; products become human and people become objects. Reification has been total. The New Left Idea defined cultural hegemony as not simply capitalism's domination over the workplace and the distribution of ideas, but rather it extends to the realms of value formation, the development of expectations and attitudes, and the creation of fears, taboos, happiness and pleasure. In short, cultural hegemony under advanced capitalism means domination over the structure of personality.

The economic attribute of the sales effort is the general expansion of demand and mass consumption. With the tendency for rising surplus as the central feature of monopoly capitalism, advertising becomes an essential force in the absorption of that surplus. Advertising is not simply a quirk of the American sociological makeup or of corporate competition but a major element in the overall stability of the economic system. Without it, economic crisis would become a regular feature of the capitalist landscape.

Part of the rising surplus is absorbed by the increased consumption stimulated by what Baran and Sweezy refer to as "civilian government." Monopoly capitalism is plagued by an inability to reach full capacity production due to its non-competitive nature and the system's failure in generating enough "effective" demand. Civilian government helps create more demand.

> "This creation of effective demand can take the form of direct government purchase of goods and services, or of 'transfer payments' to groups which can somehow make good their claims for special treatment. . .".[1]

Hence, through application of many basic "Keynesian" principles, particularly continuous deficit spending at the federal budget level, the monopoly capital economy increases effective demand and overall consumption. The increased consumption continues the absorption of the inevitable overproduction.

Without the role of civilian government as a consumption catalyst, monopoly capitalism would be unable to absorb the rising surplus. The normal pattern and interplay of private interests would fall short of the necessary effort. As Baran and Sweezy stated:

> "The structure of the monopoly capitalist economy is such that a continually mounting volume of surplus simply could not be absorbed through private channels; if no other outlets were available, it would not be produced at all. What government absorbs is in addition to, not subtracted from, private surplus."[2]

Baran and Sweezy list "militarism and imperialism" as the remaining forms of surplus absorption presently employed by monopoly capital. American militarism and imperialism, contrary to a popular myth, is not generated by a fear of socialism and the loss of economic outlets. Even socialist nations carry on economic relations with

---

[1] Ibid., pg. 143.

[2] Ibid., pg. 147.

capitalist societies. American imperialism is a function of corporate America's fear over losing the upper hand in dictating the conditions of trade and commercial affairs.

> "What they want is monopolistic control over foreign sources of supply and foreign markets, enabling them to buy and sell on specially privileged terms, to shift orders from one subsidiary to another, to favor this country or that depending on which has the most advantageous tax, labor, and other policies -- in a word, they want to do business on their own terms and wherever they choose."[1]

American imperialism is an essential feature of the political economy of monopoly capitalism and although its actual operation may be made with reference to military, political or cultural exigencies, its continued existence maintains an economic imperative.

The economic necessity of American imperialism requires a large military stockpile. Aside from the arms sales to "friendly" regimes, the American military machine must be prepared for direct intervention against revolutionary movements in "exploited countries." The giant U.S. corporations, the oligopolies of monopoly capitalism, are directly served by the existence of large amounts of military expenditures.

> "The private interests of the oligarchy, far from generating opposition to military spending, encourage its continuous expansion."[2]

---

[1] Ibid., pg. 201.

[2] Ibid., pg. 209.

97

The oligopolies have found military spending to be a direct source of capital infusion and state subsidization.

Seymour Melman presented a more comprehensive explication of the general scope and direction of the military dimension under monopoly capitalism. In his Pentagon Capitalism, Melman asserts that the military-corporate establishment is well beyond categorization as a "military-industrial complex."[1] The size of military spending and the degree of influence the Pentagon maintains over its corporate recipients implies that the symbiotic relationship between the federal agency and the corporate clientele must now be referred to as "state management." Melman argues that a military-industrial complex is based on market relations and incentives which produce a commonality of interests between pentagon officials, corporate managers and political elites. A military-industrial complex is essentially an alliance among these interests. However, the present model of state management is founded on the assumption of the merger between the governmental and private corporate realms with the state apparatus absorbing their corporate clients. Although this consolidation is not a legal or structural one, the real effect of the actual management of the military establishment and the handling of its defense contracts results in the state domination of private corporate decision-making. Further, Melman argues that for almost all of the major contractors, defense contracts comprise a significant factor in their overall economic stability. These corporations through the limited competitive demands of the oligopolistic market structure are forced to rely on this giant purchaser -- consumer --of their services.

The emergence of the giant military establishment has a dramatic influence on "effec-

---

[1]Seymour Melman, Pentagon Capitalism (New York: McGraw-Hill, 1970).

tive" demand and expanded consumption. Military spending averages approximately 10% of the nation's growing gross product. In addition, it has become a vital source of technological development through the government's subsidization through contracts, loans, etc., which directly benefit military production but also have a significant spillover effect on non-military production as well. The consolidation of pro-military spending advocates into a state management apparatus has the effect of increasing its overall political influence and significantly increases its probability of continued growth. It has become a major source of surplus absorption through increased consumption and investment, and it is an essential feature of late capitalism.

The role of the State under monopoly capitalism is now a more direct one as the necessities of civilian government and the military establishment indicate. However, the social programs of one may conflict with the military programs of the other as the dialectical tensions of late capitalism begin to manifest themselves. As the rising surplus places greater demands on government for increased expenditures, the required tax revenues will be more difficult to sustain. Paraphrasing James O'Connor, a "fiscal crisis of the state" may ensue.[1] O'Connor defines the fiscal crisis as the ". . . tendency for government expenditures to outrace revenues. . .". He places that problem squarely in the context of the surplus absorption needs of monopoly capitalism by arguing, ". . . it is a fact that growing needs which only the state can meet, create even greater claims on the state budget."[2] The fiscal

---

[1] James O'Connor, "The Fiscal Crisis of the State," Socialist Revolution, Vol. 2, no. 3; James O'Connor, "Inflation, Fiscal Crisis, and the Working Class," Socialist Revolution, Vol. 2, no. 2 (March-April, 1972).

[2] James O'Connor, Fiscal Crisis of the State (New York: St. Martin's Press, 1973) pg. 2.

crisis is caused directly by the inherent contradictions of monopoly capitalism. The tendency
towards overproduction and a rising surplus require a massive state effort to absorb the over-
load which has placed incredible pressure on the
revenue raising capacity of the government.

Fiscal Crisis of the State

In addition to the consumption stimulus
rendered by state intervention into the economy,
monopoly capital seeks the social capital of the
state for other purposes. Modern capitalism is
dependent on the state for the socialization of
the costs of social investment. Much of this type
of investment can directly increase the total
productivity of the economic system through the
provision of technological progress and in general
the growth of social constant capital. The highly
complex administrative and technical aspects of
advanced capitalism require major investments in
scientific and bureaucratic projects which are
necessary for an entire economic system. As
O'Connor stated:

". . . the monopoly sector . . . demands
increasing numbers of technical and administrative workers. It also requires
increasing amounts of infrastructure
(physical overhead capital) -- trans-
portation, communication, R & D, education, and other facilities. In short,
the monopoly sector results in more and
more social investment in relation to
private capital."[1]

The exigencies of oligopolistic competition -- cost reduction instead of price competition -- demand constant productivity increases
from labor and the state now provides massive
revenue required to underwrite this necessary
infrastructure, essential for the continued growth

---

[1]Ibid., pg. 24.

of the productive forces. The costs of this infrastructure would be prohibitive if undertaken by any single firm or industry.

Under late capitalism the state is charged with several major functions. Its social welfare expenditures are necessary for the stimulation of demand and consumption as well as performing those indispensable tasks necessary for the general increases in the productivity of labor and the protection of corporate profit margins. The state's military expenditures provide additional supports for technological development, productivity gains and profit and loss subsidization. In addition these military expenditures expand consumption through the general maintenance of governments friendly to American corporate demands. Modern capitalism requries the state to provide simultaneous welfare and warfare complexes for the continued growth of productive forces and avoidance of major economic crises, particularly those arising from over-production.

Monopoly Capitalism has qualitatively revised the role of the state within the capitalist mode of production. Previously competitive capitalism demanded the state's protection of the existing relations of production and the indirect and limited assistance in the growth of the productive forces through socialization of the costs of social investment. However, the modern epoch has so changed the intensity of the state's role, and the degree of government intervention into the capital accumulation process is now so profound, that a qualitatively new role has been carved out for the state sector under late capitalism. The state is simultaneously charged with the responsibility of a major intervention in the accumulation process while the state must also intervene in the orchestration of the system's legitimization process. Late capitalism requires major state intervention in both the mode of production and the mode consciousness development.

These concomitant functions of the state lie at the foundation of its "fiscal crisis." The demands made of the state's treasury from a variety of social interests are greater than the state's fiscal capacity and consequently political and economic tensions begin to surface. Monopoly capital requires more and more sophisticated technological and administrative advancements in order to sustain the contemporary patterns of growth. Monopoly capital seeks those appropriate social investments and expenditures of state funds in securing that growth. Other strata, particularly those outside the mainstream of economic progress -- the unemployed, welfare clients, etc., -- are demanding social expenditures which will not appreciably increase overall productivity or effective demand. In addition, the state is under continued pressure to conduct its business with greater productivity and more mileage per tax dollar. This latter aspect of the crisis will directly challenge workers within the state sector. The various interests among the monopoly, competitive and state sectors will check over the amount and direction of state expenditures and overall state policy.

According to O'Connor the short run solution to the fiscal crisis of the state will entail dramatic increases in productivity within both the state and monopoly sectors. Monopoly capitalism will demand income expenditures on the "social" (welfare) industrial complex, most particularly on those projects which will increase productivity and lower production costs in their respective industries. In addition the state will be forced towards greater economy and productivity, directly challenging the administrative workers of this sector. It will be state expenditures which essentially promote "social harmony" among the marginal economic populations that comprise the welfare and unemployment roles as well as some unskilled labor categories. This will allow a greater state role in the growth of the accumulation process and maintain its efforts in the surplus absorption process, while it simultaneously reduces the scope of its legitimization effort. Consequently state revenues can be realigned with state expenditures. By the state's abetting the growth of monopoly capital, its expenditures generate a revenue return -- increases in the state's tax base. Legitimizing expenditures allocated to the marginal population sectors of society do not offer so direct a return. As O'Connor wrote:

> "The hoped-for long-term effect of the more rapid development of the social-industrial complex is an increase in productivity throughout the economy . . . thus expanding total income and the tax base and easing the burden of financing the budget."[1]

The political effect of this solution is the awakening of antagonisms among a variety of previously dormant social groups. State employees and their clients will be directly confronting a frontal assult by monopoly capital and the state. In addition, a variety of workers in service-related industries will similarly suffer from the new direction of the social industrial complex. O'Connor's analysis leads to the conclusion that the poor, the marginal workers, and may members of what the New Left identified as the "new" working class would be thrown together in a political coalition against the vested interests of the state and monopoly sectors. Regardless of the outcome of this political struggle the role of the state under late capitalism will remain intertwined with the monopoly sector of the economy, continuing the state's necessary function in the accumulation process, and probably history will witness its intensification.

Late Capitalism and the Post Accumulation Era

The general character of late capitalism had been described by some American New Leftists

---

[1]Ibid., pg. 221.

as one of "disaccumulation."[1] The foundation of this concept was initially introduced to the New Left in Marcuse's One Dimensional Man.

> "The technological change which tends to do away with the machine as individual instrument of production, 'as absolute unit,' seems to cancel the Marxian notion of the 'organic composition of capital' and with it the theory of the creation of surplus value . . . Now automation seems to alter qualitatively the relation between dead and living labor . . .".[2]

Marcuse conceptualizes a system of capital accumulation principally emanating from the technological rather than the labor realms of the work process. He suggests an intermediate mode of production that bridges capitalism and socialism.

Several New Left authors borrowing and building on Marcuse suggested that "late capitalism" is qualitatively distinct from competitive capitalism because it is no longer built on an "accumulation" process. They understood the relative reduction in the level of socially necessary labor in the expansion of goods production as the end of "accumulation" and the emergence of "disaccumulation."

---

[1] Most importantly: Martin Sklar, "On the Proletarian Revolution and the End of Political-Economic Society," Radical America, Vol. 3, No. 3, March-June 1969; and Karl Klare, "The Critique of Everyday Life, The New Left, and the Unrecognizable Marxism," in D. Howard and K. Klare, The Unknown Dimension: European Marxism Since Lenin, op cit. pgs. 3-33.

[2] Herbert Marcuse, One Dimensonal Man, op cit., pg. 28.

". . . the relationship is one of capital accumulation so long as an increased
production and operation of means of
production requires an increased employment of living human labor-power
measured in man-hours of socially necessary labor."[1]

This process is transformed when the expansion of
goods production is not accompanied by an increase
in labor power.

"In other words, disaccumulation means
that the expansion of goods production
capacity proceeds as a function of the
sustained decline of required, and
possible, labor-time employment in
goods-production."[2]

What precisely is the meaning of "accumulation" and "disaccumulation"? What exactly
is being accumulated? Labor? Profit? Capital?
Sklar seems to imply that capitalism is a system
of labor accumulation while Marx asserted it was a
system of capital accumulation. Marx had no dif-
ficulty accounting for increases in technology and
the productivity of labor. The basic relationship
of the system was based on the antagonistic roles
of capital and labor. Sklar had the system accumulating the latter instead of the former -- an
analytic concept which requires a comprehensive
review of Marx's economic and social theory.

Moving beyond these initial problems of
definition, the "disaccumulation" argument had
some analytic merit. It attempts to clarify the
wedding of the cultural and economic domains under
late capitalism. As Shapiro wrote:

---

[1] Martin Sklar, op cit., pg. 9.

[2] Ibid., pg. 9.

105

"Not only did scientific technology begin to displace the proletariat as the primary productive force, but the technification of direction and control through the buraucratization of enterprises as well as the intervention of the state into the economy and the introduction of capitalist planning represented new forms of self-regulation of capitalism as a political system."[1]

With the decline of surplus labor, cultural hegemony and its consequent reified social patterns become the regulator of the political economy of late capitalism. Social control is now cultural rather than political. Political supremacy is enforced through technological domination and the cultural assimilation of one dimensionality.

Conclusion

The American Student Movement of the 1960's conceptualized late capitalism as a system of "corporate liberalism." Particularly significant is the intensified role of the state apparatus in the accumulation of capital and the growth of the productive forces. The new state functions are directly related to the problems of surplus absorption generated by the tendency of surplus to grow. In addition, the exigencies of oligopolistic competition and growth require significant cost reductions and consequently the state must play a crucial role in the underwriting of the required social investments in public goods that dramatically affect the overall status of productivity.

From the New Left analysis one maintained that the state role carries with it an

---

[1]Jeremy Shapiro "One Dimensionality: The Universal Semiotic of Technological Experience" in P. Breines, Critical Interruptions, op cit., pg. 146.

106

important dimension of social control and cultural hegemony. The continuance of a compatible public philosophy and the maintenance of ideological justifications for policy decisions are compatible with this intensified state function. The state must also maintain a constant battery of expenditures which ameliorate social injustices and essentially serve as legitimization functions. Finally the state maintains important aspects of the cultural apparatus which are significant in the formation of social consciousness, but ultimately its constant reliance on a technological rationality becomes its most important weapon in this area.

Further the New Left Idea lead to the conclusion that the state's technological rationality simultaneously justifies the primacy of efficiency and the undemocratic values of professionalism. It maintains the ideological superiority of "things," which is quite compatible within a cultural milieu set in the commodity form, and it concommitantly establishes the political and ideological superiority of privileged groups in the decision-making process surrounding the entire system.

The identification of the hegemonic functions of the liberal state -- political, economic, and cultural -- was a major aspect of the New Left Idea. In addition, it attempted a significant breakthrough in the deterministic [and astrological] character of the doomsday marxism of the "orthodox" Old Left. In sum, the New Left political economy was linked to the concepts of cultural hegemony and personality development that would continue the development of a new praxis, highlighting the common fabric and dialectical force between political economy and its ideological foundation in everyday life.

107

Chapter Five
Class and the Question of Agency for Change

The intellectual stalemate of the Fifties was rooted in the contrasting positions confronting the American radical: the deterministic projections of the orthodox marxists maintained the hopes of old visions and older logic, while former marxists were proclaiming the final stage in the assimilation of the American working class into the fabric of the "mixed economy." C. Wright Mills seemed alone in his search for new agencies - white collars, social scientists, youth, et al. Within that beleagured search for agencies and movement the origins of the American New Left are found. The tactical orientation of the American Left was no more than apparent in that period. Its theoretical understanding of developed capitalism deprived of any significant review of the post war situation, the American Left agonized over the loss of its old agency and began the search for new ones. The Left approached theory as if the theoretical and historical anaylsis required in the assessment of capitalism's modern tendencies were only fringe ornaments to be hung on existing political movements in order to rationalize and beautify them.

Perhaps this should not have been unexpected. The symmetry of the Old Left logic was firmly entrenched in the revolutionary terrain. Leninism and social democracy had elevated the working class beyond the point of analysis and consequently theoretical development had long since been precluded in the American marxist milieux.[1] Any recognition of the realities of

---

[1]Richmond op cit. has a long discussion of the Old Left's - social democratic and communist - reliance on foreign models for political analysis. The former relying on their understanding of the German Social Democratic Party and the latter on the Bohshevik Party. In each case, working class

working class politics would inevitably be met with either a withdrawal from marxist and neo-marxist politics - as with Daniel Bell and many other "pluralists" - or a new expedition would begin to uncover new social groupings and agencies for change. Within this context the New Left's search for an agency was commenced - in backward fashion, practice defered by its lack of theory.

To the Old Left the conceptual understanding of the working class lost its historical context. The working class became a category frozen in history, to be thought of only as a monolithic entity possessing a common experience and consciousness. It was beyond theoretical and empirical scrutiny, surrounded by a variety of astrological projections concerning its imminent political promise. In fact the greater the assimilation of unions - the traditional political organ of the working class - into the bureaucratic fabric of monopoly capitalism, the more bizarre and disjointed were the Old Left descriptions of working class consciousness and political tendencies. The New Left's constant search for agency and later its theoretical contributions concerning late capitalism and everyday life were at the very minimum important because they re-affirmed the subjective nature of the working class role in political movement as described in Marx's writings. The New Left Idea reasserted the historical specificity of Marx's description of the working class. Once this was understood by the American New Left, it was capable of proceeding with its theoretical task and it began its more comprehensive project - an analysis of modern capitalism, contemporary social consciousness and the construction of a new praxis.

---

consciousness would simply develop in accordance with either reform oriented parliamentary politics or workplace organizing. Also see James Weinstein, The Decline of Socialism in America, 1912-1925 (New York: Vintage Press, 1967).

The Theory of the New Working Class

The writings and ideas of three French radicals had a major impact on American New Left writers' and, for a time, on the American Student Movement's rethinking of the role of the working class. Alain Touraine, Serge Mallet and Andre Gorz were the major developers of the theory of a "new" working class.[1] This new concept became popular in the American Students for a Democratic Society (SDS) between 1966-1967, and it offered that movement a brief moment of political self-identity quite distinct from its former and future identities.

The new working class was defined as those workers involved in the technical domain of advanced capitalist society. These are the workers who have become the "overseers" of automated capitalism - the technician, the engineer, the bureaucrat, the professional. The new working class is above all educated labor, scientifically trained labor. In the American context the new working class is used simply to describe university-trained strata of the work force.[2]

---

[1] See, specifically, Serge Mallet, La nouvelle classe ouvrier (Paris: Editions du Seil, 4th Edition, 1969); Andre Gorz, Strategy for Labor (Boston: Beacon Press, 1967); Alain Touraine, Post Industrial Society (New York: Random House, 1971).

[2] Some interesting observations on the impact of the new working class theory are contained in an important article on the subject written by Stanley Aronowitz that first appeared as a paper at the ocialist Scholars Conference 1970, and reprinted in an anthology. See, Stanley Aronowitz, "Does the United States Have a New Working Class," in Fischer, ed., The Revival of American Socialism, op cit., pgs. 188-216.

The new working class is politically motivated not by the quantitative demands associated with the traditional economist posture of organized labor, but rather by its orientation toward the qualitative demands that essentially revolve around control of the work process. The foundation of this new theoretical concept rests on an essentially different concept of socialism and the character of modern capitalism. According to Mallet:

> "Behind the conflict between 'qualitative' and 'quantitative' demands lay a difference in the conception of socialism in a developed country, and of the respective roles of the party, the union, and the initiative of the workers."[1]

Mallet's analysis is an attempt to trace the current development of the productive forces and assess their influence on the political viability of a variety of actions in the production process.

> "In the last analysis, it is not a question of knowing whether or not there exists a working class, but of knowing what are the vanguard forces within it, those which have the possibility of formulating clearly the future of the workers and those which because of their objective situation, cannot psychologically go beyond their present conditions."[2]

Mallet bases his projections of the vanguard role of the new working class in traditional marxist categories. He argues, however,

---

[1]Serge Mallet, op cit., pg. 23, quoted in D. Howard, "New Situation, New Strategy: Serge Mallet and Andre Gorz," in Howard and Klare, The Unknown Dimension, op cit., pg. 391.

[2]Ibid., pg. 391.

that class is not a monolithic entity possessing a unified consciousness and ideology as orthodox marxism has consistently projected. Rather the working class is composed of a variety of forms from the past and present development of the productive forces.

Analysis, then, must be founded on the changing character of the capitalist mode of production; that is, the new working class analysis must rest on the current status of Marx's organic composition of capital:

". . . because of the increasing investment in constant capital (plant, equipment, and the like) and the decreasing investment is variable capital (labor power), capitalism will necessarily have to cut its circulation (distribution) costs in order to increase its profit while at the same time and for the same reasons, capitalism also will have to produce more and more goods in order to pay for its continued expansion, and it will, therefore, need an ever large force of non-productive laborers whose only task is distribution."[1]

This analysis fit easily into the New Left concept of monopoly of late capitalism. Howard's point can be integrated with Baran and Sweezy's description of the imperatives of surplus absorbtion under late capitalism. O'Connor's predictions of the increased stress on the state sector are also easily linked to Howard's statement because monopoly capitalism requires significant growth within its infrastructure as it moves towards a more automated and technological stage which requires more massive social investment and bureaucratic administration. In short, the New Left political economy was based on the notion that the more centralized and technologically sophisticated the mass consumption and production

---

[1] Ibid., pg. 392.

character of capitalism, the greater its vulnerability to its inherent weakness of disproportionality. Modern capitalism is a highly interdependent complex set of production and consumption processes, and as it moves toward a rising organic composition of capital - less labor to produce at even greater output levels - modern capitalism is more and more concerned with the problems of consumption and surplus absorption. Under modern capitalism disproportionality is a crisis of underconsumption. The effect of these developments is the rise of a new working stratum - perceived by Mallet and others as a new working class - which is centrally concerned with distribution and consumption. In this sense, the strategic location of this new technical strata presents itself as a vanguard position.

Late capitalism is a highly technological and bureaucratic society. To the new working class theorists what appeared as auxiliary occupations - service industries - are now prime parts in the overall functioning of the system. The technical stratum of society is an historical entity, born of the distinct features of monopoly capitalism. Its central purpose is the movement and consumption of goods. Within the context of one dimensional society, the domination of personality by reified labor, the circulation of goods and the desublimation of previously forbidden instinctual needs demonstrates that consumption has simultaneously emerged as a new form of social control and private profit. Although the dominated personality originates in the everyday submission required in the relegation of labor into the commodity form, the New Left Idea identified the hegemonic role of consumption under late capitalism.

The new working class theory attempted the reaffirmation of the historical specificty of any class description and it outlined the various historical movements and distinct character of work relations as well as the working class under different stages of capitalist development. To the new working class theorists capitalism had experienced three distinct movements: the transitional period characterized by the worker as dispossessed artisan; the emergence of competitive capitalism and its mass production forms; and finally the rise of the highly technical and automated features of corporate liberalism where the worker is essentially an overseer of the production process. All of these movements and work patterns may co-exist at any particular stage of capitalism; however the modern epoch is marked by the near obliteration of the dispossessed artisan, the gradual decline of the assembly line worker and the rise of the automated overseer. In short, the new working class theorists concluded that the organic composition is constantly rising and the previous forms of work are diminishing, allowing for the new vanguard role of the new working strata. As Dick Howard wrote:

"The relation among the three movements of industrialization can best be defined in terms of the change in the organic composition of capital . . . As we enter the third movement of development, however, the situation is aggravated; the percentage of investment in variable capital is very small; . . . The state has to aid business by building infrastructures . . . The needed 'rationalization' of the home market is provided by the now famous 'one dimensional' consumer."[1]

The new working class of the previous epoch is now the old working class of the modern period. To Mallet the new working class of late capitalism is composed of the overseers of production and the "technicians," - mostly concerned with distribution and the overall infrastructure - or superstructure - of the entire system. According to Mallet the educated laborer responds to the irrationality of the capitalist work process quite differently from his predecessors of the competi-

---

[1]Ibid., pgs. 396-397.

tive period. Instead of settling for simply wages, or employment benefits, etc. - Mallet and Gorz assert that the new working class of late capitalism demand qualitative changes in the overall work process. Their position and training within the work process leads them to demand greater control over the work process itself. They are as concerned with the democratic character of the production system as they are with the remunerations and protections afforded them.

The new working class theory not only is founded on the severe rise in the organic composition of capital but also in the assumption that modern capitalism is approaching the possibility of "post scarcity" environment - that is, the technological capability will soon exist, given the appropriate political economy, so that the basic material needs of society could be met in total. The gradual recognition of this fact - particularly by the new working class - marks the general erosion of traditional capitalist values and a move away from the capitalist praxis of modern society towards a more creative alternative. As Andre Gorz wrote in A Strategy for Labor:

> "For capitalist civilization, efficiency, productivity, and output have always been the supreme 'values'; these 'values' now reveal themselves in their true light: as a religion of means. They could find their justification in the midst of acute scarcity by making possible an intense accumulation of the means of overcoming scarcity. In the midst of disappearing scarcity, they become a religion of waste and of fictitious opulence."[1]

Eventually these two value system conflict:

---

[1]Gorz, op cit., pg. 127.

"They could co-exist only if dehuman-
ization in work were strong enough to
make the workers unfit for any but
sub-human and passive leisure and consumption. Such is no longer the case."[1]

The Marcusean "qualitative leap" is now a possibility.

Different from Mallet and Gorz, James
O'Connor argued a quasi new working class position
in The Fiscal Crisis of the State. O'Connor
asserted that the exigencies of surplus absorption
and cost efficiency ubiquitous to developed capitalism will result in severe fiscal demands placed
on the state sector by monopoly capitalists while
the marginal populations of surplus labor will
place equally severe competing fiscal demands for
welfare oriented benefits. This crisis will
result in the State's attempts in a reduction in
social welfare expenditures and a simultaneous
assault on State workers in pursuit of significant
productivity increases. To O'Connor the crisis
would forge a worker-client alliance, which is to
say an alliance of the surplus population against
monopoly capital and the State sector. O'Connor
concluded that only a massive cooptation of this
movement by the State and its monopoly clients
would allow for the further stability and growth
of the system as we now know it. This "new"
reform was termed by O'Connor as the social-
industrial complex.

"An alliance of a majority of the surplus population, especially if it were
supported and to a degree defined by
radical state worker organizations [new
working class - R.G.] would have great
impact on American economic and political development. Perhaps the only way
for the state to contain such a movement

---

[1]Ibid., pgs. 127-128.

116

is to accelerate the growth of the social-industrial complex, which combines the voting power of the surplus population with money and power of significant groups of monopoly capitalists and state contractors."[1]

Whether or not advanced capitalism will be able to ameliorate its contradictions through a new intensified reform, it is clear that Mallet, Gorz, O'Connor, et al., outlined the political importance of the new technical strata for the continued stability of modern capitalism. Whether or not they constitute a new class or simply a previously neglected aspect of the old class is less important than the New Left's identification of their existence and importance in the modern political economy. The significance of this "new" agency flows directly from the qualitatively altered character of developed capitalism where the superstructure and its state, cultural and scientific domains have become primary dimensions in the continuance of capital accumulation instead of the seemingly auxiliary role to which they had been demoted within "orthodox" Old Left thought.

University Intellectuals and Students

The New Left placed a prime emphasis on the political role of intellectuals and students who, according to Mallet, constitute parts of the new working class. Intellectuals for the most part are found in universities. Monopoly capitalism more than ever is dependent on ideological hegemony that universities and intellectuals contribute to the cultural apparatus and the entire superstructure. They provide important roles in the overall shaping of values and interpretations of social and scientific phenomena.

---

[1] O'Connor, op cit., pg. 245.

117

In addition the unique nature of late capitalism requires the organization and growth of a knowledge industry. It needs a constant source of legitimization but now, as importantly, the oligopolistic nature of the economy and its reliance on a sophisticated bureaucratic infrastructure has necesitated the continuous flow of data and analysis that will afford monopoly capital greater control of the market. To the new working class theorists the knowledge industry aided in the overall rationalization of the marketplace which is so critical because of the sharp interdependence of monopoly capitalism and its consequent vulnerability to spontaneous lapses in underconsumption or overproduction. The university provides an important source of such knowledge for modern society because its intellectual diversity allows for a constant review of all factors that affect market relations - political, economic, scientific, cultural, sociological and anthropological. The university becomes the factory of the new knowledge industry.[1]

Factories - knowledge or otherwise - must be organized in a distinct fashion. There must be hierarchically arranged relationships in the production of knowledge. The academic chain of command essentially fulfills this function. It is able to inflict punishments and extends rewards for the appropriate levels of knowledge production and complementary behavior patterns. Within the multiversity funded research and publication become important yardsticks of productivity. The sources of funds are from the State sector or the monopoly sector, funneled through a variety of agencies and "private" institutions, serving the vesting interests of both.

---

[1]The following section of this manuscript and succeeding chapters will specifically outline this New Left argument with a review of the major literature pertinent to the development of the New Left Idea.

Not only does the knowledge factory provide adequate control over the level, productivity and direction of knowledge, but it simultaneously trains the new strata of educated labor that will soon be in charge of the scientific and administrative apparatus of the superstructure. In short, the knowledge factories - multiversity through semi-vocational - concomitantly produce necessary knowledge in the rationalization of a sensitive market and train the apprentices that will supply the growing superstructure with the continuous flow of educated labor - "old" and "new" working class strata.

The new working class theorists contended that the politicization of the university under modern capitalism brings with it the politicization of university intellectuals and students. These social groups - intellectuals and students - are forced into playing new roles under modern capitalism and these new roles are subject to change with alterations in the productive forces and the relations of production. The New Left Idea projected intellectuals and students into the mainstream of the modern political economy as a distinct productive stratum in addition to its pre-existing role in the production of a hegemonic capitalist praxis.[1]

---

[1] Marx outlined the ideological role of intellectuals as a hegenomic force under competitive capitalism. See, Marx and Engels, The German Ideology, op cit. In addition, Lenin also indicated the importance of intellectuals and students in the overall revolutionary movement. See, V. I. Lenin, What Is to be Done, (New York: International Publishers, 1969). The New Left's stress on the productive role of intellectuals is outlined also in the writings of tne now popular Antonio Gramsci. See, A. Gramsci, The Modern Prince and Other Writings (New York: International Publishers, 1970); Antonio Gramsci, Prison Notebooks (New York: International Publishers, 1972). In addition, see John Cammett, Antionio

The New Left Idea reopened the question of "class" for marxist theory. This follows directly from its political, economic and cultural critique of advanced capitalism. However, the development of the various analyses did not flow in the orderly manner in which they appear in this manuscript. Its initial concern was more popularly the question of agency. The New Left defined and redefined its political, economic and cultural analyses as various American New Left movements - most particularly the Student Movement - agonized over a variety of tactical and strategic questions whose answers required a full-fledged theoretical synthesis and an outline of a new praxis.

Conclusion: The New Left Idea and the New Praxis

It is my contention that the New Left Idea is bound by the development of the three concepts: cultural hegemony and the critique of everyday life, the emergence of monopoly capitalism, and the reassessment of the historic agency for change. The Idea was an attempt to spawn a new praxis that would transcend the reproduction of the existing social patterns and political heirarchies of capitalist organization, which were maintained in the praxis of the Old Left. The historical importance of the New Left is not simply measured by the success of its movements but rather the questions it raised for marxist theory marked the mergence of the question of an appropriate praxis for modern American capitalism. The New Left Idea challenged important apsects of the Old Left's interpretation and application of Marx and Engels in the advanced Western nations.

Gramsci and the Origins of Italian Communism (Stanford: Stanford University Press, 1967); Eugene Genovese, "On Antonio Gramsci," Studies in the Left, vol. VII, No. 2, March-April 1967, reprinted in James Weinstein and David W. Eakins, ed., For a New America (New York: Vintage, 1970).

It is my conclusion that the New Left Idea identified the cultural hegemony and domination of personality as a historical development necessary for the survival and gorwth of late capitalism. The emergence of corporate liberalism is characterized by its dependence on the cultural apparatus for the manipulation of the personality in the corporate pursuit of the mass market. The conquest of the personality by monopoly capital leads to the political integration of the working class. The New Left Idea described the near complete homogenization of labor through the domination of culture and the structure of personality. The severe sensitivities generated by monopoly capitalism's unique interdependent economic arrangement and its system of administered prices and non competitive techniques demand the constant growth of a massive market - a market only possible through the careful nurture of a fetish for commodities in lieu of the satisfaction of the creative instincts more natural to the personality.

The Student Movement was not a self conscious realization of the New Left Idea. Any attempt to define the New Left Idea must include a description of the Student Left in order to achieve a more accurate description and assessment of the unique historical significance of the New Left Idea. Although the Idea and the Movement were many times disparate, ignorant of one another, theory without practice and vice versa, each did influence the other since ultimately each sought juncture with the other. Theory sought practice, and the Movement constantly sought definition and direction. In this sense, each was somewhat aware of the other, feebly seeking contact and many times horrified when they found it.

PART TWO:

THE AMERICAN STUDENT MOVEMENT 1960-1968

The history of the Student Movement in the sixties is not simply a history of Students for a Democratic Society (SDS). It is much more than that.[1] During its initial stage, much of the Movement is, in fact, SDS; however, as the Movement developed, a popular base it extended well beyond the borders of any of its organizational structures. But the mainspring of the intellectual vitality of the Movement was to be found within its own institutions, most particularly SDS.

The late fifties were marked by a growing Civil Rights Movement in the South and a small but visibly active Peace Movement. Student political activism during the late fifties was focused on the struggle for radical integration and the control of the nuclear technology of modern warfare. The Southern Christian Leadership Conference (SCLC), the Congress of Racial Equality (CORE) and the Student Peace Union (SPU) were among the major organizational expressions of these movements.

The SDS was the youth group of the Student League for Industrial Democracy (SLID), which itself was the youth group of a long-standing social democratic organization, the League for Industrial Democracy (LID). The latter group claimed numerous well-known members, past and

---

[1]This introduction is intended as a simple chronology of the Student Movement. For a detailed history of the events involving SDS and the Student Movement see among others, K. Sale, Op cit.; Teodori, op cit.; Jacobs and Landau, op cit.; and James O'Brien, "The Development of a New Left in the United States, 1960-65" (Ph.D. Dissertation, University of Wisconsin, 1971).

present, not the least of whom were Jack London, James Farmer, Bayard Rustin, and Michael Harrington. Since World War II, LID and SLID were breaking ground for many contemporary liberal, reformist political leaders and academic personalities. In 1959 SLID organized a new youth offspring which was blessed with the title of Students for a Democratic Society. Intended as a campus research and discussion oriented effort, SDS quickly veered away from LID's outline of its purposes. Under the early leadership of Al Haber, a Michigan University graduate student, SDS became an activist organization as well as a citadel for the discussion of the main issues on the contemporary American scene. By 1961 Tom Hayden, then a young undergraduate at Michigan, joined forces with Haber. These two unique personalities traveled a good portion of the South and North, reviewing the Civil Rights Movement and the response to it on numerous Northern campuses. Their efforts quickly increased the size of SDS and, to be sure, extended the LID vision of its purposes.

By the time SDS presented its first manifesto, The Port Huron Statement, its allies in the League for Industrial Democracy were becoming quite uneasy with Haber and Hayden's perspective on the Cold War and the direction of student activism.[1] At the Port Huron Conference, the two central issues of debate between the insurgent SDS leadership and the LID activists were in Michael Harrington's words, ". . . Communism and American Liberalism."[2] In the Port Huron Statement SDS

---

[1] Students for a Democratic Society, The Port Huron Statement, S.D.S., 1962, available from the Wisconsin Historical Society, Madison, Wisconsin.

[2] For Harrington's account of the early New Left Student Movement see, Michael Harrington, Fragments of the Century (New York: Saturday Review Press, 1973). See also Kirkpatrick Sale, op cit.; and see, Unger, op cit.

initially declared its critical review of American liberalism, which led directly to its separation from the social democratic section of the Old Left heritage.

SDS's initial activism was concerned with participation in the Southern Civil Rights Movement. By 1963 SDS developed its own political program. It formed the Economic Research Action Program (ERAP) which was a Northern community organizing effort aimed at mobilizing the white poor and eventually developing the white component in a new interracial movement of the poor. Soon after the 1963 March on Washington, organized by a variety of civil rights groups, SDS's ERAP program began with a modest number of project sites. The two most well-known efforts were in Chicago, where the project was named Jobs or Income Now (JOIN), and in Newark, New Jersey, under the title, The Newark Community Union Project (NCUP). By 1965, however, all of ERAP was in disarray. The program was geared to the issues of unemployment and local control, but SDS was unable to establish anything approaching a mass base.

With the collapse of the ERAP program, the new focus of SDS and the Movement as a whole was the Vietnam War. In 1964 at the University of California at Berkeley, a coalition of various political groups protested the University's decision to censure political activity on campus. The Free Speech Movement (FSM) became the stereotype of student protest on the campus for the decade of the sixties. The FSM identified the complicity of the educational establishment with the corporate elite and the governmental apparatus, hence with the dominant political institutions in a society characterized by institutional racism, economic inequality, and a militarist outlook. The campus became a major arena of political activism to the Student Movement after the Berkeley protest. In March 1965 SDS organized the first major antiwar march on Washington. Much to everyone's surprise an estimated 25,000 people demonstrated their disapproval of American involvement in the Southeast Asian conflict. Paul

Potter, President of SDS, addressed the assemblage, urging his audience to "name the system" that produced Vietnam and Selma. By the fall of 1965 at a second demonstration, attended by 100,000 people, Carl Ogelsby, president of SDS, characterized the system as "corporate liberalism." SDS and the Student Movement now went beyond reform. Rejecting the traditional notions of patchwork liberal programs to ameliorate the ills of American society, SDS called for a radical restructuring of the political economy. From 1965 the imperialist critique of American society became popularized within the movement, and in general a broader analysis of developed technological society began to emerge.

Within the Civil Rights Movement a growing separatist critique was developing. The Student Nonviolent Coordinating Committee (SNCC) declared that the efforts of white activists should center exclusively in the white population. The slogan of "Black Power" was popularized by 1966. Having suffered a major tactical setback with the failure of the ERAP program in the North, the White Student Movement withdrew from the Civil Rights Movement in the South. The student focus was now on foreign policy.

The Anti-War Movement was made up of a variety of formal and informal groups such as The Committee to End the War (CEW), the MOBE and New MOBE committees, and SDS itself. Important aspects of the Movement were draft resistance and national demonstrations to end the war, and attacks on the university for complicity with the war effort. By 1967 numerous campuses experienced student protests on these issues and programs. It was clear by 1968 and the events surrounding the Chicago convention of the Democratic Party that the Student Movement was moving well beyond a critique of foreign policy. It was now concerned with something approaching a social and political revolution.

The post 1968 period of the Student Movement was characterized by the search for radical strategies for change. Within SDS two major factions existed side-by-side. One was the Worker-Student Alliance Caucus. This was for all practical purposes the child of the Old Left, the then Maoist, Progressive Labor Party. Its program sought a "leave the campus" version of the Old Left's proletarian style. The other major faction considered itself more "new left", rooted in an insurgent revolutionary youth culture and intent primarily on supporting the liberation movements of the Third World and Black America. This second faction eventually named itself the Revolutionary Youth Movement (RYM I). In 1969, these two forces clashed at the SDS convention, resulting in the collapse of the organization, each claiming legitimacy to the organization's title. However, both were condemned to obscurity by the early 1970's. RYMI ultimately became Weatherman, an isolated terrorist group, and the WSA-PLP formation faded from the political scene.

From 1969 to 1971 the Student Movement was without any significant national organization. Its political life was doomed by the failure of another organization to emerge and replace SDS. However, even without national coordination the Student Movement was able to produce its most intense protest during the weeks surrounding the American invasion of Cambodia in the spring 1970. With the failure of this national student strike to end the Indochina War and given the intensity of the government's repressive "war" on domestic dissent (Kent State, the Chicago Seven, et al.) the Student Movement soon passed from the stage of American politics.

In this decade of turmoil, the Student Movement was guided by numerous political critiques and strategical directions. Each of these was a significant event in the intellectual history of the New Left Idea in the American context, which form the substance of this section.

Critics have asserted that the New Left Student Movement lacked an adequate intellectual foundation. In fact the popular myth that now surrounds the assessment of this contemporary movement identifies the major cause of the New Student Left's political collapse as its general lack of intellectual development and its overall theoretical poverty, Accordingly, the absence of ideas and the distrust of the intellectual process and rational discourse prompted the Student Movement to adopt a political scope and an ideological vision set in a utopian and anarchistic posture, where the explanation and analysis of difficult and confusing public issues were glossed over in favor of the short-term resolution of personal troubles.[1] In this view, the New Student Left is portrayed as a movement without significant ideas and prey to unclear utopian apparitions as surrogates for lucid political analysis. The failure of the Student Movement was not a failure of ideas but rather a failure to develop ideas. So the explanation goes.

Historian Christopher Lasch portrayed the New Student Left experience as one devoid of ideas. He wrote:

"Too often the new left confused dogma with ideas and tried to live without

---

[1] Among a variety of authors expressing this view Irving Howe seems to have become their stereotype. In the summer 1965 issue of Dissent, he wrote, "Some of them [New Leftists] display a tendency to regard political - and perhaps all of - life as a Hemingwayesque contest in courage and rectitude. People are constantly being tested for endurance, bravery, resistance to temptation, and if found inadequate, are denounced for having 'copped out.' Personal endurance thus becomes the substance of, and perhaps even a replacement for political ideas." See Irving Howe, "New Styles in Leftism," reprinted in Jacobs and Landau, op cit., pgs. 291-2.

them, preferring pure intentions to clear thinking."[1]

This sweeping generalization is the singular perception of the Student Movement popularly projected in the contemporary literature. Although there is much variation on the specific reasons for the collapse of the Student Movement, intellectual poverty is most frequently cited. Lasch and others have attempted to explain the sixties and its movements as anti-intellectual assaults on corporate capitalism which were destined for historical brevity and political obsolescence because of their lack of direction, unity, and vision - all products of an intellectual poverty and its political correlatives of barren strategies and futile tactics.

The American New Left Student Movement did indeed produce ideas. In fact, as long as it remained a New Left movement, the Student Movement made significant contributions to the development of a contemporary critique of corporate liberalism and it provided important redirections for the American marxist focus. However, the Student Movement was not an artifact of the New Left Idea - or vice versa. The Movement and the Idea were separate entities that shared a common terrain and experienced occasional junctures in their respective histories. The Student Movement's contribution to an understanding of the New Left Idea occurs at these points of intersection where theory and practice were brought together, producing specific moments in the development of a new American Marxist praxis. The failure of the Movement does not diminish the Idea but rather points out its undeveloped character and the overall failure to integrate theory and practice.

---

[1]Christopher Lasch, "After the New Left" in C. Lasch, The World of Nations (New York: Vintage Books, 1974). This essay originally appeared in The New York Review of Books, October 21, 1971.

The deterioration of the Student Movement is in
part related to the absence of these intersections
in sufficient enough quantity to sustain a growing
movement caught in the rush of events. But the
collapse of the New Student Left was not a function of the failure to produce ideas, per se, but
rather its demise was more an inability to produce
ideas that would sustain vitality and gain a
measure of acceptance.

The purpose of this section is to contest the
predominant view of the New Student Left by outlining its intellectual contribution and, secondly, to identify the juncture of these ideas with
the larger theoretical foundation of the New Left
Idea. In short, this section of this manuscript
seeks the intersection of theory and practice.
What I am attempting to do is what John Higham, a
noted intellectual historian, wrote in the following succinct manner:

> "The logical consistency of a sequence
> of thought, the elaborations of a world
> view, the achievement of a reverberating
> insight, or the power of an idea to bear
> further intellectual fruit - these
> become the norms of an intellectual
> history pledged to the sheer creative
> vitality of the human mind."[1]

The Student Movement & Political Style

The critiques of everyday life and late
capitalism, coupled with a renewed search for a
social agency for change, are the central concerns
of the New Left Idea. All these concerns have a
direct correlation to significant aspects of the
practice of the New Left Student Movement. However, neither the practice of the Movement nor the
development of the Idea is a replication of the

---

[1]John Higham, <u>Writing American History</u> (Bloomington: Indiana University Press, 1970), pg. 32.

other, and quite plainly, much of the practice represents the antithesis of the Idea. But a definite New Left motif exists in the practice of the Student Movement between 1960 and 1968, and the basic failure of the New Left Student Movement was its inability to maintain its coherence with the New Left Idea.

Before outlining the main ideas of the Student Movement it is essential to attempt the rediscovery of the mood and context of Student Movement practice. The intellectual atmosphere and political ambiance of the Movement were important variables contributing to the intellectual vitality of the student environment and paradoxically explain its anti-intellectual tendencies. Within a movement where form was so important that it often became synonymous with substance, mood and style many times were crucial to the development of ideas and sometimes became their surrogate. The Movement was characterized by style and a vision distinct from that of the Old Left but unfortunately it was unable to discard completely the political liabilities and intellectual drawbacks of its American marxist and neo-marxist heritage. The Student Movement uniquely sought a political environment marked by full participation and non-exclusion for all the variants of American radicalism. In fact these two principles were direct descendants of the "totalistic" scope that the movement sought. Social change was envisioned not only as institutional rearrangements in the social structure, but also as personal change.

The expectation of a "new man" arising from the movement was a continuous goal of the student struggle. The Movement itself was to be educator and civilizer for an entire generation - at least this was the hope of its early leadership. They clearly identified the crucial relationship between personal life and social consciousness and it was their belief that the Movement would become the intervening force which would allow people to make connections between "public issues and personal troubles." The Student Movement sought a transformation of both the public and private

131

realms believing that this "total" approach to political development was crucial for significant social change.

> "The emphasis in the movement on 'let-
> ting the people decide,' on decentral-
> ized decision-making, on refusing al-
> liances with top leders, stems from the
> need to create personal and group iden-
> tity that can survive both the tempta-
> tions and the crippling effects of this
> society. Power in America is abdicated
> by individuals to top-down organiza-
> tional units, an it is in the recovery
> of this power that the movement becomes
> distant from the rest of the country and
> a new kind of man emerges."[1]

For these reasons the Movement's emphasis on the forms of democratic participation and its belief in the principle of non-exclusion constituted important aspects of its politics and clearly identified the importance of the rituals of daily life for the maintenance of the political status quo. The practice of the Student Movement re-flected the crucial dimension of the New Left Idea: that the substantive foundation of late capitalism is now critically dependent on the forms of social interation; and, that even within a "desublimated" environment the cultural patterns and social forms are crucial elements in the maintenance of the commodity form and market structure that encases all human experience under corporate liberalism. In short, a significant portion of the New Left Student Movement style reflects the critique of the hegemonic role of modern culture under late capitalism. Clearly, the Movement failed to work out the full theoret-ical meaning of its position and certainly it never was expressed in such terms; however,

---

[1]Tom Hayden, quoted in Paul Jacobs and Saul Landau, op cit., pg. 110.

Hayden's statement sums up an entire dimension of the Student Movement experience which is usually absent from analyses of the cultural history of the Movement. The crucial failure of the Movement was its inability to maintain a balance between the public and private domains, and, finally, falsely identifying the latter as morally superior to the former. Having correctly identified the hegemonic role of culture and daily life, the Movement lost sight of the psychological limitations placed on the structure of personality by the contemporary socio-economic framework.

Unfortuantely, the written contribution of the Student Movement was always short of the growing need for ideological development. It appears as the need for a comprehensive political analysis became more evident, the narrow individualistic focus on personal problems and changes enjoyed an even greater popularity within the Movement. Eventually this phenomenon - always present in the Student Movement - developed into a full-blown anti-intellectualism and ultimately into a suicidal revival of the most vulgar and naive caricatures of "revolutionary theory."

Early in the SDS experience, Al Haber, first President of SDS, identified this trend when he was debating the merits of the northern community organizing projects of the mid-sixties. He wrote:

"I am highly critical of the substance of such community work because it has been without radical direction, clarity of goals, or significant differentiation from liberal reform. And I am critical of its organizational role because it diverts us from more important things, ignores our role as a student organization and has become the base for an unfortunate anti-intellectualism in SDS . . .".[1]

---

[1] Al Haber quoted in Kirkpatrick Sale, op cit., pg. 110.

Haber understood the ideological shortcomings of this trend and its likely effect on the viability of the movement's future. He was also aware of the fact that SDS wasn't simply putting off educational programs and intellectual development but creating a politics whereby direct experience was weighted as morally superior to intellectual growth.

> "The 'in the ghetto' enthusiasm has become linked with an anti-intellectualism, a disparagement of research and study, an urging of students to leave the university, a moral superiority for those who 'give their bodies,' etc. 'In the world' has become to mean 'in the slum.' Beside being slightly sick, this suggests a highly perverted analysis of American society. . ."[1]

Jacobs and Landau also commented on this tendency when they wrote in 1966:

> "The majority of the newer SDS members, unlike the founders, are not well read in Marxism or in the other radical literature. Most of them - middle class born and bred, not oriented toward careers - are moved to action primarily by events in their own lives, and they see themselves as active public men."[2]

The problem of internal education coupled with the growing environment of anti-intellectualism fostered a distinct political style that denigrated theory; consequently Movement strategies and tactics became more disjointed and spontaneous. This is not to argue that political analysis was abandoned or even that this tendency impeded the

---

[1] Ibid., pgs. 110-111.

[2] Jacobs and Landau, op cit., pg. 29.

work of particular intellectuals. It did, however, disrupt the earlier symmetry between ideas and actions evident in the first years of SDS. Consequently the conjunction of theory and practice became more difficlut to maintain during the latter days of the Student Movement. The trend continued in the face of questions confronting the Movement which called for more precise strategies concerning questions of constituency, system and consciousness. As long as direct experience would be perceived as "morally superior" to intellectual growth and internal education, the Student Movement's style would retard its political effectiveness and reduce its historical significance.

However, within the Student Movement, there was a clear understanding of this need for ideological coherence and theoretical maturity. In fact, in some quarters, intellectual development was perceived as a goal of the Movement and a prerequisite for its political success. This position was clearly outlined in an important exchange that appeared in Studies on the Left in the spring, 1965. There, the editors divided sharply over the focus of the Movement in light of the collapse of the northern community organizing conducted by Students for a Demcoratic Society within its Economic Research Action Program. On one side Tom Hayden, Norm Fruchter and Alan Cheuse were arguing for a continued effort in the poor white communities while on the other side, Stanley Aronowitz, James Weinstein, Eugene Genovese, and several others asserted the need for a broader constituency base and the construction of a sophisticated analysis involving and explanation of political consciousness under advanced capitalism. As the latter group wrote in an editorial reply to Hayden and company:

> "Yet if a significant movement is to be built it must be around a coalition large enough at least in theory, to contest for political power. Every group of potential allies should be explored. Programs of action should be developed to facilitate connections

135

between the various components - including the poor - when they become sufficiently conscious to engage in explicitly political action. Such a coalition needs a common view of the existing society, common programmatic demands (or at least complementary ones), a common vision of a new form of social organizations designed to satisfy human needs. We feel it is necessary to begin the theoretical work on which such a movement can be based."[1]

As long as an anti-intellectualism was present in the Student Movement, its attainment of ideological and theoretical sophistication would be prevented - and with them, the strategy and tactics of Movement practice would remain disjointed and finally, they would become random. In the last years of the New Left Student Movement part of it turned to an adventuristic isolated terrorism that was rooted in the assumptions of the impossibility of mass political change and of the impentrability of mass consciousness. Part of it reverted to the archaic rhetoric of a previous period, resurrecting the frozen images of marxism whose death was initially procalimed by the birth of a "new" left. Marx's indictment of the latter phenomenon seems most appropriate.

"Men make their own history, but they do not make it just as they please; they do not make it under circumstances directly encountered, given and transmitted from the past. The tradition of all the dead generations weighs like a nightmare on the brain of the living. And just when they seem engaged in revolutionizing themselves and things, in creating some-

---

[1]Stanley Aronowitz, James Weinstein, Lee Baxandall, Eugene Genovese and Helen Kumer, "Reply," Studies on the Left, Summer, 1965, reprinted in Jacobs and Landau, op cit., pg. 274.

thing that has never yet existed, precisely in such periods of revolutionary crisis they anxiously conjure up the spirits of the past to their service and borrow from them names, battle cries and costumes in order to present the new scene of world history in this time honoured disguise and this borrowed language."[1]

So, too, at the height of its influence the Student Movement reverted to the pursuit of irrelevance. As Murray Bookchin wrote, "All the old crap of the thirties is coming back again . . .".[2]

Yet between the reformist orientation of the early SDS and the Student Movement's latter day schizophrenic dualism of dogmatic Leninism and Narodniki terrorism lay an intellectual foundation that was coherent with the outlines of the New Left Idea. Specifically, the main ideas of the Movement correlated with the basic categories of the New Left Idea: the critique of cultural hegemony and everyday life, a beginning analysis of the unique character of modern capitalism, and the search for new agencies for social change.

---

[1] Karl Marx, The Eighteenth Brumaire of Louis Bonaparte (New York: International Publishers, 1963), pg. 15.

[2] Murray Bookchin, Post Scarcity Anarchism (Berkeley: Ramparts Press, 1971), pg. 173. This quote comes from an essay included in the book but previously widely distributed within the Student Movement in May, 1969, under the title "Listen Marxist."

Chapter Seven

Cultural Hegemony, Everyday Life, and the Student Movement

From its birth the intellectual dimension of the Student Movement sought to identify the sociological juncture between public institutions and personal comportment. The Movement always maintained a focus on the political nature of personal life, that is to say, it was seeking an explanation and analysis about the central paradox that confronted the post World War II American radical: the relationship between political consciousness and daily life.

The initial outline of this totalistic focus of the "new" left appears in the founding document of the Students for a Democratic Society (SDS), its <u>Port Huron Statement</u>.[1] This document can now be understood as more than an organizational manifesto because its coherence with the New Left Idea is explicit, especially with regard to personal consciousness, its socio-economic context, and its identification of the social forces thought capable of restructuring the contemporary institutaonal framework.

The introduction to the <u>Port Huron Statement</u> was entitled "Agenda for A Generation" and it began:

"We are people of this generation bred in at least modest comfort, housed now in universities, looking uncomfortably to the world we inherit."[2]

Quite unlike the documents of Old Left organizations, this manifesto proclaimed its student identity and took recognition of the growth in the

---

[1] SDS, <u>op cit</u>., pg. 1.

[2] SDS, <u>Ibid</u>., pg. 1.

living standard of most Americans. This in itself was a step forward from the doomsday rhetoric of the Communist Old Left - rhetoric that was reminiscent of the industrial revolution and working class pauperization.[1]

In its essence the document was an indictment of liberal ideology and cold war policy. It sharply outlined a number of empirical contradictions that confronted post war liberalism: the empty egalitarianism demonstrated by poverty amidst affluence, blatant racism in the face of the "political democracy" and the "primacy" of human rights, and technological development threatening economic instability and the myth of upward mobility. As the authors state:

> "While these and other problems either directly oppressed us or rankled our consciences and became our own subjective concerns, we began to see complicated and disturbing paradoxes in our surrounding America."[2]

In contrast to Daniel Bell and the other "end of ideologists," the Port Huron Statement asserted that the United States was gripped by a fundamental crisis that demanded a sense of urgency.

> "Our work is guided by the sense that we may be the last generation in the experiment with living."[3]

---

[1] The entire thrust of William Foster's Toward a Soviet America, previously cited, characterizes this Old Left position. The crisis of capitalism was imminent, revolutionaries should prepare by organizing the working class at the point of production, ready to seize power at the moment of collapse.

[2] SDS, Ibid., pg. 2.

[3] SDS, Ibid., pg. 2.

One can interpret the Port Huron Statement to mean
that the complacency of the mass of society was
not a function of the system's stability and
general consensus, but rather a portrait of
estrangement, the perception of public powerlessness, and the impenetrable nature of industrial
society.

". . . Beneath the stagnation of those
who have closed their minds to the
future, is the pervading feeling that
there simply are no alternatives, that
our times have witnessed the exhaustion
not only of Utopias, but of any new
departures as well . . . Feeling the
press of complexity upon the emptiness
of life, people are fearful of the
thought that at any moment things might
thrust out of control. They fear change
itself, since change might smash whatever invisible framework seems to hold
back chaos for them now."[1]

In this passage, the Port Huron Statement's vital link with the New Left Idea is evident. Each can be interpreted to mean that the
political and social consciousness of the mass of
society under late capitalism is characterized by
an acquiescence to the socio-economic intimidation
of th power and complexity of industrial society.
Within their everyday lives, people repress and
rechannel their sense of estrangement and are
reconciled to the fragmentation of personal and
public experience because industrial society's
concentration of economic and political power,
coupled with its appearance of impenetrability,
seems to exhaust ideas and preclude future change.
History appears to have ended, at least in terms
of mass influence over its main elements. Individuals perceive their inability to be anything
other than objects in the historic process.

---

[1]SDS, Ibid., pg. 2.

"The dominant institutions are complex enough to blunt the minds of their potential critics, and entrenched enough to swiftly dissipate or entirely repel the energies of protest and reform, thus limiting human expectancies."[1]

Further, this statement implies that this condition results in a narrow personal focus by most people, sanity and rationality demanding the forced fragmentation of social experience. The personal and the "political" core divided, the basic political stability of the system was assured. Any intellectual history can begin to detect the broader intellectual implications of the Port Huron Statement's explanation of self-estrangement within the American post-industrial epoch. Certainly the political nature of private life was its message and it further implies the importance of fragmented experience of everyday life as forms of social control. Hinting at a Marcusean interpretation of contemporary social consciousness, the document continues:

"Some regard these national doldrums as a sign of healty approval of the established order - but is it approval by consent or manipulated acquiescence?"[2]

The document is more explicit in its identification of the political importance of everyday life, as its authors state:

"The apathy here is, first subjective -- the felt powerlessness of ordinary people, the resignation before the enormity of events. But subjective apathy is encouraged by the objective American situation - the actual struc-

---

[1] SDS, Ibid., pg. 2.
[2] SDS, Ibid., pg. 10.

141

tural separation of people from power, from relevant knowledge, from pinnacles of decision making. Just as the university influences the student way of life so do major social institutions create the circumstances in which the isolated citizen will try hopelessly to understand his world and himself."[1]

Although the authors of the Port Huron Statement have not outlined a process of the biological and instinctual manipulation of social consciousness as Marcuse developed in One Dimensional Man, they explicitly argued that the magnitude of institutional power - which is to say the power of vested interests - was a significant aspect of the social psychological fabric of mass society and, in particular, that it was a significant effect on the individual's social expectations and social behavior. Coherent with the New Left Idea, the interplay of personality and political order was seen as a crucial factor in the maintenance of the existing social order.

"The very isolation of the individual - from power and community and ability to aspire - means the rise of a democracy without publics. With the great mass of people structurally remote and psychologically hesitant with respect to democratic institutions, those institutions themselves alternate and become, in the fashion of the vicious circle, progressively less accessible to those few who aspire to serious participation in social affairs."[2]

The Port Huron Statement has been portrayed in the literature as either a document reflecting the isolated student status of the vari-

---

[1] SDS, Ibid., pgs. 10, 11.

[2] SDS, Ibid., pg. 11.

ous movements of the sixties, or as a manifesto
proclaiming the movement's attack on the contradictions of cold war liberalism. Little attention
is given to this document's discussion of the
development of social consciousness under late
capitalism. In fact, the Port Huron Statement
represents a major breakthrough for the American
Left because it reopened the question of consciousness with regard to its historically
specific cultural underpinnings. It looked to the
juncture of public and private life as an
important area of political analysis as it moved
the American radical critique of society away from
its sterile heritage of simple-minded deterministic explanations of social consciousness. The
document was in part an attempt to discover the
locus of power and social control under late
capitalism and, from this starting point, it began
the search for insurgent agencies of social change
and relevant strategies and programs that would
provide the nucleus for a mass political movement.
It explicitly indicated that the patterns of
everyday life must become a part of any such
strategy.

"A New Left must transform modern complexity into issues that can be understood and felt close-up by every human
being. It must give form to the feelings of helplessness and indifference,
that people may see the political,
social and economic sources of their
private troubles and organize to change
society. In a time of supposed prosperity, moral complacency and political
manipulation, a new left cannot rely on
only aching stomachs to be the engine
force of social reform."[1]

---

[1]SDS, Ibid., pg. 63.

143

The Administered Society and One Dimensionality

A more specific account of the political relationship between the public and private domains of everyday life [1] emerged from the Berkeley student revolt of 1964.[1] That initial confrontation between insurgent students and administration of the University of California clearly set student youth against the educational bureaucracy and the "administered" university. Berkeley became the crucible of a much larger struggle involving the authenticity and integrity of the individual within the techno-bureaucratic complex which characterizes modern capitalism.

The Berkeley University administration unilaterally decided that certain university restrictions would be placed on political activities on campus. The Free Speech Movement challenged the authority and power of the administration in abridging their First Amendment rights but more importantly the FSM challenged the lack of student participation in the governance of the university. The issue of administrative censorship was not simply an issue of civil liberties to the FSM, but rather indicative of a larger political question - the absence of participatory democracy on the Berkeley campus. Mario Savio drew the analogy between the politics of the university and the politics of American society by extending his analysis from the undemocratic governance of the multiversity to the denial of participatory

---

[1] A range of literature is available on the Berkeley student revolt. Among the most informative see: Seymour Martin Lipset and Sheldon S. Wolin, editors, The Berkeley Student Revolt (New York: Anchor, 1965); Immanuel Wallerstein and Paul Starr, The University Crisis Reader, Vols. I & II (New York: Random House, 1971); Jacobs and Landau, The New Radicals, op cit.; and Kirkpatrick Sale, SDS, op cit.

democracy under advanced industrial society.[1] His
speech on the steps of Sproul Hall became the
intellectual and political benchmark across the
nation.

Savio's speech was entitled "An End to
History."[2] He argued that bureaucracy attempts to
rationalize human experience in order to evaluate
phenomena exclusively in terms of their overall
"efficiency." The only important decision-making
criterion is that which reflects on the immediate
condition of the bureaucratic institution as it
seeks the "least costly" path to achieve its
goals. "As bureaucrat, an administrator believes
that nothing new happens. He occupies an a-historical point of view."[3] The status quo and the
stability of the contemporary configuration of
power guarantee the life of the bureaucratic
institution, hence its ultimate goal of activity
becomes the preservation of itself and the contemporary environment. The past and future become
irrelevant. History has ended in the sense that
historical or dynamic analysis anticipates social
change and thus threatens the stability and efficiency of the institution. As Savio said:

> "The same is true of all bureaucracies.
> They begin as tools, means to certain
> legitimate goals, and they end up feed-
> ing their own existence. The conception

---

[1]Mario Savio was a major figure in the Free Speech
Movement, and popularly identified as its major
spokesman at the time of the Berkeley revolt.

[2]It was also reprinted in most New Left readers,
such as Treodori, op cit.; Mathew Stolz, The Politics of the New Left (beverly Hill: Glencoe
Press, 1971); Mitchell Cohen & Dennis Hale, op
cit.; Wallterstein and Starr, op cit.

[3]M. Savio, "An End to History" in M. Teodori, op
cit., pg. 159.

that bureaucrats have is that history has in fact come to an end."[1]

The institutions of the administered society must develop certain skills and attitudes among its people in order to ensure the maintenance of this very system. The personality of the individual must be coherently shaped with regard to the one dimensional world of techno-corporate bureaucracy. The administered society not only seeks political stability and a static socio-economic environment but also must fashion particular kinds of personalities in order to sustain its very life. It must educate and socialize its citizens so that their very instinctual make-up is suitable to the goals of the instutitional framework. All behavior is modified by the expectation of social conformity to the surrounding social apparatus. In short, the administered society requires personalities that instinctually recognize their inferiority in the predominant bureaucratic social complex. The role of the university in the administered society is then reduced to the socialization and credentialization, the overall "production" of students who;

". . . must suppress the most creative impulses that they have; this is a prior condition for being part of the system. The university is well structured, well tooled, to turn out people with all the sharp edges worn off, the well-rounded person. The university is well-equipped to produce that sort of person, and this means that the best among the people who enter must for four years wander aimlessly much of the time questioning why they are on campus at all, doubting whether there is any point in what they are doing, and looking toward a very bleak existence afterward in a game in

---

[1]M. Savio, *Ibid.*, pg. 159.

which all of the rules have been made up, which one cannot really amend."[1]

Savio's speech was important for two reasons. First, it had a major impact on the nature and direction of the Berkeley Free Speech Movement and the Student Movement in general. It had a direct effect on historical events. Secondly, Savio's speech developed the growing Student Movement idea that the personal and public orbits of social experience were crucially linked in the overall political framework of the American social system. Beyond simply the achievement of social control, Savio argued that the system specifically shaped the cultural vision and psychological makeup of its youth and that this socialization was a crucial underpinning of the political process.

Between the time of Savio's speech in 1964 and the spring of 1967, the Students for a Democratic Society and the Student Movement in general took a profound turnabout in its programmatic direction. As stated earlier, from 1960-1965, SDS was predominantly involved in the Civil Rights Movement and community organizing in poor white northern neighborhoods under the madate of the Economic Research Action Program (ERAP). By 1965 two fundamental conclusions were obvious to the student left. First the student wing of the Civil Rights Movement was eliminating its white component as it turned towards a black nationalist perspective. The role of the white student activity was significantly decreased if not non-existent. Secondly, the community organizing under the ERAP program was in a shambles. It had failed. Few project sites were active, and even in those, only a few hearty souls remained, desperately trying to organize a shrinking constituency.

---

[1]M. Savio, Ibid., pg. 161.

147

The New Left Student Movement might have been expected to remain an isolated strain among the mainstream currents of American politics during the 1960's. It might have faded even into obscurity, drowned in its own despair and failure. Its leaders might easily have joined the ranks of the 'left-wing' reformers within the Democratic Party, inheriting that task from their 'parental' benefactors of the League for Industrial Democracy. But there were at least two reasons for the continuing vitality of the New Student Left in the United States. First, the characterization of the irrational nature of the American political system as expressed in <u>The Port Huron Statement</u> caught on. The Student Movement's critique of American society was founded on an empirical reality. The system was beset by poverty amidst affluence, by publics without political power. Alienation, estrangement and the fear that 'things could go out of control at any moment' were real phenomenon deeply felt by a significant portion of American youth. Under the ideological veneer of pluralism and the end of ideology, America's economic affluence and political stability seemed well assured. Yet the New Left not only exposed the vulnerability of those ideological supports in the face of widespread economic and political inequality, but it captured the fundamental contradictions inherent in the fabric of everyday life in an advanced industrial society. Whether knowingly or not the Movement's characterization of American society exposed the hierarchial nature of a technological and bureaucratic society which prided itself on its democratic order and life style.

The second reason for the survival of the New Left in the mid-sixties was the ideological contradiction inherent in the imperial character of the United States' war in Indochina. The irrationality of that foreign policy and the obvious deceptions in the conduct of that war clearly ran against the myth of a democratic foreign policy in defense of a democratic world order. American youth were clearly reluctant to defend that foreign policy much less carry it out. The revolt against the war was not so much a statement against imperialism as it was a revolt against a political system which was losing its legitimacy. The reality of life in America contradicted the promises of pluralist democracy and cultural contentment. The American government's pursuit of political control in Indochina exaggerated this contradiction and forced a response from those asked to bear its mortal and moral costs.

The focus of the Student Movement's agitation was the campus, challenging the bureaucratic apparatus of the administered university and the war in Southeast Asia. Savio's speech, and the entire Berkeley experience, became a model for future Movement practice. The administered university presented the Student Movement with a direct target for its general call of participatory democracy. The university was understood to be as oppressive and strategically important an institution of late capitalism as its industrial complex and the cultural and related apparatus of the system's superstructure. The antiwar effort, although less narrow in its focus, similarly became a campus-based and significantly campus-focused operation.

For these reasons the period between Savio's speech and the spring of 1967, was characterized by the development of a critique of corporate capitalism and its forms of social control. More specifically, it was within this period that a significant part of the movement's critique of everyday live and a more sophisticated understanding of the politics of the "personal" emerged. Savio's "An End to History" extended the initial commentary of the Port Huron Statement. From 1965-1967 the theoretical growth of the student reached out for a Marcusean interpretation of the ideological hegemony of the cultural domain of modern society. Savio brought them beyond C. Wright Mills and now several others sought to imbue the informal and loosely articulated movement critique with a Marcusean flavor.

The most significant of these attempts was a widely circulated analysis of late capitalism written primarily by David Gilbert and presented with others in a variety of forms.[1] The most popular of these various presentations was entitled, Consumption: Domestic Imperialism, which circulated as a movement pamphlet. Although this work was most closely identified as a "new working class" argument, it popularized an important extension of Savio's position and the Port Huron Statement's identification of the political nature of cultural life.

Gilbert's essay definitely attempted an integration of Marcuse and Mills with the burgeoning critique of political economy within the New Left Student Movement.[2] Consumption: Domestic Imperi-

---

[1] The basic idea was printed in pamphlet form as David Gilbert, Consumption: Domestic Imperialism (New England Free Press: Somerville, Mass.). However a similar position also circulated within the Wisconsin Draft Resistance Union as: Bob Gottlieb, Gerry Tenney and Dave Gilbert, The Port Authority Statement, presented at Princeton University to the Radical Education Project (REP) Conference in 1967; also in shorter form as: Dave Gilbert, Bob Gottlieb and Gerry Tenney, "Toward a Theory of Social Change in America," New Left Notes, May 22, 1967. Although most importantly a document associated with the Student Movement's adaption of the "new working class" analysis, it has significance for its cultural critique as well.

[2] Gilbert's paper developed the idea of the administered society beyond the previous efforts. He not only identified the manipulative nature of the socialization process but he specifically linked this hegemony to the vested interests of the corporate state. Gilbert argued that the human needs are defined by the cultural apparatus as it perverts the instinctual makeup of the human personality. He wrote, "The basis for creating

alism formally injected the categories of marxist and neo-marxist scholarship into the political dialogue of the Student Movement during the mid-sixties. It attempted to integrate this critique into a general political strategy but found that these concepts were not easily translated into a workable practice that promised a mass movement. Indeed, as will later be discussed, the critique of everyday life is still too undeveloped to serve in a programmatic fasion.[1]

He extended his critique of the manipulation of need qua commodity to a larger analysis of the necessity of this process for rationalization of the economic marketplace and stability of the system. The

". . . management of demand is crucial to the survival of modern capitalism. Waste production concommitant with the management of demand amplifies the notion of exploitation as appropriation of labor and extends the notion of exploitation into the sphere of consumption."[1]

---

and manipulating consumer needs is using and redirecting real human needs, associating them with a given commodity. Thus the needs for sex, love, personal identity and creativity, etc., are used to sell products with which they have no necessary connection." (pgs. 7, 8)

[1] The contemporary presentation of a "counter" culture has not been projected as the embryonic vision of the future post-industrial society, but rather its image has harkened back to the paupered images of a pre-industrial world. However, Gilbert's position paper did not identify a specific "cultural" strategy, but rather extended a growing critique into its larger socio-economic framework.

[2] Ibid., pg. 9.

Gilbert introduced the general New Left motif by linking the new forms of social control and personal estrangement with the qualitative changes in the character of modern capitalism. His analysis developed the initial comments of the Port Huron Statement on alienation and personal isolation, but he retained its essential quality which was its reconciliation of the two dimensions of the historical process - the public and private orbits of human experience. Gilbert wrote:

> "In short, exploitation under modern capitalism is the difference between potential social productivity and over-all quality of life (including both work and consumption.)"[1]

In attempting an analysis that retained a "totalistic" character - Gilbert joined the exploitation of labor in the work process with the conditions of estrangement, isolation and boredom dominant in the private dimension of everyday life. This "new" movement critique of modern American society suggested the necessity of a broader strategy.

> "Unlike the 30's, strategy can no longer be based on material demands alone (wage demands in reaction to economic crisis). Rather, it must be based on a more encompassing projection of the social and economic alternatives to the status quo."[2]

Gilbert's essay was a popularization of a variety of previously stated positions,[3] never-

---

[1] Ibid., pgs. 9-10.

[2] Ibid., pg. 13.

[3] The most obvious of these are Marcuse's work on that point, in addition to Serge Mallet, Andre Gorz and Lee Baxandall.

theless it synthesized and homogenized them into a readable and influential position. At approximately the same time Lee Baxandall wrote a significant article that appeared in Liberation in April, 1966, entitled "Issues and Constituency of the New Left."[1] Similarly his piece emphasized the growing importance of non-material issues to the New Left Student Movement. The thrust of the Baxandall's article was an attack on the narrow economistic vision of traditional American marxism. He called upon radicals to "contemporize the socialist perspective." Baxandall stated his basic thesis in the following manner:

"I submit that all issues relevant to building a major Left constituency must be domestic, emerging from daily experienced repugnance and needs; and these issues must be located decisively beyond the 'Magenfragen' [material issues] which, however nostalgically, must be foresaken as issues since the Establishment effectively controls them."[2]

Baxandall argued that material issues could appeal only to the underclass, those ghettoized citizens on the fringes of American prosperity. SDS, he continued, cannot hope for a mass socialist movement because this constituency will be absorbed into the fabric of modern American society. Unfortunately SDS approached this constituency without even those issues that promised material improvement but rather the programs seeking "participatory democracy." To Baxandall this was the correct issue but the wrong group. Instead, those potential agencies for social change unconcerned with material insecurity - "the unoriented students, educated" and other such

---

[1] Lee Baxandall, "Issues and Constituency of the New Left" in Liberation, April 1966.

[2] Ibid., pg. 21.

groups - are the appropriate groupings whose primary concern is with their feelings of estrangement and isolation. These constituencies, which Baxandall believed comprised the mass of society, can be politicized and organized around the "fundamental failures of American life to be democratic, and to be beautiful."

Baxandall's article was a direct call for the Student Movement to abstain from the temptation of making imperialism the center of the Student Movement in favor of focusing student political efforts on the contradictions confronting people in the ". . . fundamental and daily experienced issues that the Establishment cannot begin to remedy."

The arguments of Baxandall and Gilbert reflect the growing presence of Marcuse in the intellectual development of the Student Movement.[1] However encouraging their analyses appeared for the genuine theoretical advancement of the movement up to that time, the concept of ideological hegemony in daily life experience was never translated into a workable programmatic expression and, consequently, into a new praxis. The New Student Left reduced the critique of daily life from a potential catalytic program for a working and middle class constituency to a mere issue intermixed with a distinct political style. It mearly simplified the concept to a matter of personal style in the evasion of the dominant cultural patterns.

---

[1] It should remain clear, however, that the Student Movement was never a Marcusean movement. As Paul Breines wrote in "From Guru to Spectre: Marcuse and the Implosion of the Movement," Paul Breines, ed., Critical Interruptions (New York: Herder & Herder, 1972); "Before proceeding it should be made clear that the Movement, above all in this country has never been a 'Marcusean' movement . . .," pg. 6.

The Personal Is the Political

Perhaps the most influential factor in its failure to develop the critique of cultural hegemony into a viable political program was the Student Movement's acceptance of the position that personal change must either be experienced prior to, or simultaneously with, institutional change. As the goal of the movement evolved from its reformist orientation to a radical and ultimately revolutionary perspective, changes in personal qualities, behavior and demeanor were to become equivalent in political significance with the broader programs and movements seeking institutional reconstruction. As the movement aged, it not only sought "community" within the larger social fabric, but it went beyond simply seeking individual changes in consciousness and moved towards the general demand for individual and personal purity. To paraphrase the earlier excerpt from the Port Huron Statement, the Movement did not merely expect the evolution of a "new man" amidst the gradual but escalating struggle for a new social arrangement, but it now expected the "new man" to precede the new society. Eventually this psycho-political dialectic led to the position where individuals were the Revolution. Karma overtook movement.[1]

---

[1] It is crucial to understand the roots of this fetish with individual change. In one sense, its existence within the Movement reflected the very failure to grasp the concept of ideological hegemony and to reproduce it in a feasible programmatic form. This is quite different from the position of many New Left critics who totally dismissed the theoretical concept of hegemony and its contemporary political significance by pointing to the Student Movement's aborted attempts at integrating the "counter culture" into its overall perspective. Theory cannot be dismissed by misplaced practice.

From its very inception, the Student Movement was concerned with the intersection of the public and political change, believing that both were indispensable for fashioning a new society. It was only in its later years that this gave way to a notion that personal change must precede political activity. As John Judis wrote in a significant article on this subject:

> "During this period, one's understanding of 'political activity' (the attempt to create a diverse movement) was subordinated to the other (the attempt to change one's life). This led to the illusions characteristic of social utopianism: seeing our own activities as a model of revolutionary change that will spread through the society without a conscious attempt to understand our own needs in the context of the needs of other strata of the society; seeing ourselves as superior to other groups in the society; and finally, among many, believing that the complex difficulties of our lives - difficulties about our relations to each other and about what we are going to do with ourselves - could finally be resolved through our particpation in communes, small groups, collectives, through moving to the country, or into radical communities. For many, the period did awaken new possibilities. But for others the end result was disappointment and dissillusionment."[1]

The chronological account of the origins of this imbalance between the personal and political domains is difficult to chart. However, the

---

[1] John Judis, "The Personal and the Political," Socialist Revolution, Number 7 (Vol. 2, No. 1), January-February 1971, pg. 28.

1965 SDS convention held at Kewadin, Michigan stands as a benchmark of sorts. Younger, politically less experienced, unfamiliar with the history of SDS and the Left, the new activists participating in the national organization were characterized as ". . . more individualistic, as well; some said at the time even 'anarchistic' - something of the populist tradition clung to them."[1] They urged decentralized structures within the national office of SDS in order to insure individual control and influence over national decisions.

In response to this growing attitude at the Kewadin convention, Richard Flacks, a representative of the "old guard" of SDS, the inner circle that helped shape the organization during its earlier years, presented a working paper that attempted to outline the balance between personal change and political activism. His paper, "Some Problems, Issues, Proposals," was more of a centrist position at the convention and reflected the broader attitude. In his paper Flacks saw the Movement as attempting two goals. "One, which we might call existential humanism, is expressed by the desire to change the way we, as individuals actually live and deal with other people."[2] The second is directed at the "radical transformation of the social order." Flacks argued that the Movement must embrace both of these goals.

Flacks went on to condemn the imbalance between the two that was now beginning to favor 'personal troubles' over public issues. He wrote:

"Involved too is an overpersonalization of the Movement, a situation in which

---

[1]Sale, Ibid., pgs. 206-207.

[2]Richard Flacks, "Some Problems, Issues, Proposals" reprinted in Jacobs and Landau, op cit., pg. 163.

one's personal needs and hang-ups are increasingly acted out in the larger arena, and attempts at solution of these take precedence over more collective concerns. The necessary distinction between the public and the private self breaks down, with the likely result that either the community is undermined or personal freedom is sacrificed in order to preserve the community."[1]

Flacks argued that there are occasions where the two goals are incompatible with one another. Compromise is an important element of political communication; however this involves personal sacrifice and limitation. The goals will always involve a common tension within the movement, and a balance is struck, according to Flacks because the tension: "is in most of the participants" and because representatives of each orientation will both belong to the movement. "We must embrace the poet and the saint," Flacks concluded, "but we must keep a necessary distance from them."

Richie Rothstein, an ERAP organizer in Chicago during the mid-sixties, identified this fetish with the personal domain as a major factor in the collapse of participatory democracy within SDS itself. In a working paper presented in 1971 to the membership of the New University Conference (NUC) entitled, Representative Democracy in SDS, Rothstein argued that in the name of reform, numerous changes were made within SDS to destructure its internal organization. These reforms were ostensibly opposed to the elitism and hierarchy supposedly prevelant in SDS from the Kewadin Convention up until the final demise of SDS in the Summer of 1969.[2] However, Rothstein stated that

---

[1]Ibid., pg. 164.

[2]Richie Rothstein, Representative Democracy in SDS (Chicago: New University Conference, 1971).

these very arguments urging decentralization of decision-making, the dismantling of the national office, and the general demand for "collective" and not electoral forms of governance reduced political responsibility, accountability and participation and ultimately resulted in greater elitism and hierarchy. In short, in an attempt to integrate the personal and political into the central arteries of the Student Movement - its organization apparatus - the Student Movement elevated the personal concerns, attitudes and general dispositions above the general political programs, issues and needs of the movement and its constituencies. The personal **became** the political.

From Kewadin 1965 until the collapse of SDS due to its internal split between the Old Left oriented worker-student alliance wing and the anarcho-terrorist Weatherman section, the fetish for personal liberation through political deed grew in geometric proportions. One response was for individuals to dismiss personal liberation and return to the rigidities of the vanguard party form of political organization. The Progressive Labor Party and its SDS faction, the Worker-Student Alliance were the major benefactors of this trend. Here personal change was a secondary concern because truth was identified exclusively within the working class experience. The other response was the elevation of personal experience beyond political accountability. This faction drifted toward the Revolutionary Youth Movement within SDS. For them acting as revolutionaries took precedence over any objective calcualtion of building a mass movement.

The New Left Student Movement succeeded in identifying the social junction between the private and public domains of contemporary life. The Movement established - to a minor degree - a semblance of intellectual contact with the New Left Idea's political critique of everyday life under late capitalism. The Movement's realization of the political significance of this domain of modern life was a major breakthrough for American marxist and neo-marxist praxis. The inclusion of the repressive role of the cultural apparatus into the left politics of the modern period is what made it "new."

Simultaneously with this major advancement of modern Leftism, the failure of the Student Movement to project its critique of cultural life into something that resembled an analytic overview with a programmatic expression was an equally major setback. It resulted in the isolation of its student constituency from its natural allies within other strata of society. The failure to popularize a fullblown critique of the role of cultural hegemony either in general or class terms was a failure to translate the New Left Idea into a "popular" idea. Whether or not this was a function of the power of "repressive desublimation" of modern industrial society as identified by Marcuse or a function of the subjective character of the movement itself, is a question to be delt with in the final chapter. But it is quite ironic - and tragic - that the most theoretically developed dimension of the New Left Idea is its rediscovery of the hegemonic role of capitalist culture and yet the most notable intellectual failure of the Student Movement was its inability to establish a meaningful program for this concept.

Chapter Eight
The Student Movement and the Concept of
Advanced Capitalism

More developed than its exploration of cultural hegemony was the Student Movement's critique of contemporary capitalism. With respect to the corporate nature of liberal ideology and the changed role of the state there was considerable correspondence between the New Left Idea and the Movement's focus. The Student Movement played a particularly important role in popularizing the imperialist thrust of American foreign policy. Nevertheless, the Movement failed in developing a theoretical framework for its activity and often misapplied whatever ideas it had developed. Most of the Movement's action was, in fact, spontaneous.

It is no exaggeration to conclude that the subjective element significantly limited the achievement of the movement as much as objective conditions impeded any radical upsurge during a period of continuing prosperity and economic growth.

The initial appearance of the Student Movement's critique of contemporary capitalism was introduced in the Port Huron Statement as a generalized overview of some of the more obvious contradictions of advanced capitalism.

"The tendency to overproduction to gluts of surplus commodities, encourages 'market research' techniques to deliberately create psuedo needs in consumers - we learn to buy 'smart' things, regardless of their utility - and introduces wasteful 'planned obsolescence' as a permanent feature of business strategy."[1]

---

[1] SDS, op cit., pg. 14.

This statement outlined some problems with the economy, but did not locate their cause within the nature of the political economy.

The authors were ambiguous about the role of the state apparatus. For instance, the authors wrote:

"In short, the theory of government 'countervailing' business neglects the extents to which government influence is marginal to the basic production decisions, the basic decision-making environment of society, the structure or distribution and allocation which is still determined by major corporations with power and wealth concentrated among the few."[1]

The clear implication is that of the neutralized state apparatus and the independent corporate structure. However, the document contains further statements which imply a more interdependent relationship between the private and public sectors of the economy.

"The most spectacular and important creation of the authoritarian and oligopolistic structure of economic decision-making in America is the institution called 'The military-industrial complex' by former President Eisenhower, the powerful congruence of interest and structure among military and business elites which affects so much of our development and destiny."[2]

Finally, the Port Huron Statement includes an assessment of the effect of automation and cybernation on the structure and future of

---

[1]Ibid., pg. 14.

[2]Ibid., pg. 16.

American capitalism. The authors asserted that this new phenomenon in technological advancement was "destroying whole categories of work" while the technocratic managerial elite casually dismissed the importance of this "structural unemployment." SDS asserted that automation resulted in severe dislocation problems and the inevitable obliteration of unskilled job categories. The poor and underclass would suffer the most distressing effects of this irrational form of economic progress, where the "potentiality for abundance becomes a curse and cruel irony. . ."[1] In addition, the number of workers employed in industrial production relative to the overall employment level was decreasing.

> "More important perhaps, the American economy has changed radically in the last decade, as suddenly the number of workers producing goods become fewer than the number in 'non-productive areas' - government, trade, finance, services, utilities, transportation."[2]

The Port Huron Statement hinted at a neo-marxist view of the workings of contemporary American capitalism in its identification of structural crisis of overproduction and the systemic problem of underconsumption. As the portion of industrial workers declined in the face of cybernetic advancement and overall productivity gains, the statement reads, production gravitates towards a surplus glut and new occupational categories concerned with the distribution of production emerge and expand. In addition, it implied an integral economic relationship between soaring government spending for military production and the growing enclaves of poverty spread throughout the affluent society. Although the document did not develop an assessment of the nature of the state's role in advanced capitalism,

---

[1] Ibid., pg. 18.

[2] Ibid., pg. 20.

at least it alluded to the dramatic rise in the military sector and identified this trend as in some way structural to the economy as a whole. In general, the Port Huron Statement drew together specific economic relationships and, in so dong, laid the foundation for the broader economic analysis that emerged at a later time in the Movement's history.

One year following the Port Huron Statement, SDS produced a second manifesto, America and the New Era, intended as a further development of its political understanding of modern society and its proposed agendas for radical organization and activity. Kirkpatrick Sale described it as "less impressive than the Port Huron Statement, in part because it comes after, but also because of its narrow focus."[1] The thrust of the document was to summarize the nature of the contemporary American economic crisis of stagnant growth and chronic unemployment. It framed its economic critique within a narrow political setting, concentrating mostly on the major formal institutions of the U.S. governmental apparatus.

The initial section of the paper outlined three major features of the stagnation/unemployment crisis: (1) poverty and the maldistribution of income; (2) the arms race and the maldistribution of resources, and (3) oligopoly and the maldistribution of power. Poverty condemned a fifth of the population to the hopeless cycle of misery and moreover denied the economy of significant proportion of consumer demand. Characterized by new sophisticated technological innovations, the arms industry expanded production but maintained the same employment levels. In addition the inordinate proportion of social resources allocated to military purposes denied the economy the necessary social expenditures required to ameliorate the decaying conditions within the urban centers of modern society. Finally, the emergence of the concentration of

---

[1] Kirkpatrick Sale, op cit., pg. 90.

economic power within most American industries directly contributed to the stagnation crisis. Specifically, oligopoly has resulted in administered prices and predetermined profit rates at lower production levels. Also, oligopoly has meant that the wholesale introduction of automation into the American economy has been fashioned to fit the private aims of the corporate elite meant the destruction of jobs and the extension of income inequality.

The authors of America and the New Era characterized the nature of the stagnation crisis as an inherent feature of modern capitalism. They imply that the structural makeup of this system is plagued by the incidence of underconsumption and that this problem is directly traceable to the system's foundation on income inequality, the concentration of economic and political power, and the distribution of resources. The authors asserted that the political apparatus is geared toward the creation of a corporate state where the economic coordination and overall planning of the system will be manipulated and guided by the governmental apparatus for the primary purpose of meeting the needs of its corporate component at the expense of the public interest.

"Internally, the New Frontier is moving toward the image of the 'corporate state,' following such countries as France and West Germany, in which government and business recognize that national planning by central bodies and strong programs of social welfare are necessary if social conflict which threatens the corporation economy and established power is to be avoided."[1]

The state under modern American capitalism was characterized by its corporate bias and

---

[1]Students for Democratic Society, America and the New Era, The Wisconsin Historical Society, Madison, pg. 14.

also by its role of corporate protector. The document did not project the state as an independent economic entity but rather as an underwriter of corporate stability and privilege. The state would intervene in the economic system to sort out "frictional troubles" but such long run problems as the concentration of power and administered prices were glossed over with cosmetic attention at best. Further, structural unemployment which results from the corporate manipulation of production schedules to sustain higher prices and profits were dealt with through the introduction and growth of welfare programs instead of an assault on corporate power.

> "It is clear that as the troubles of our economy become more acute and more visible, the administration would lean toward 'corporatist-bureaucratic' solutions rather than attempting to construct[1] institutions of democratic planning."[1]

The state is also responsible for the "systematic and unprecedented intervention in labor-management disputes." The goal of this feature of governmental activity is the control of labor. Under the banner of the public interest, the state actually represents the elite private interest of the corporate sector at the expense of the working class.

> "The thrust of this policy has been heavily in the direction of tax and other incentives and concessions to business and strongly against the use of the strike by the labor movement."[2]

The governmental apparatus manages the stagnation crisis by maintaining unemployment within politically acceptable levels while under-

---

[1] Ibid., pg. 14.

[2] Ibid., pg. 14.

writing the technological innovations of the corporate sector with a variety of subsidies, tax write-offs and investment credits. The resulting automated advances contribute to the higher levels of unemployment which the state attributes to the 'costs of increased productivity.' The governmental sector serves to legitimize the privilege of the corporate sector. It must continuously manage real and potential social conflict emanating from the irrational and unequal basis of a society that rests on the rhetoric of rationality and equality.

The nature of the economic crisis was connected with the credibility of the legitimation function of the governmental sector. Mass movements of social protest must be channelled into established institutional channels in order to maintain a stable environment for the political economy. Such insurgencies as the Civil Rights Movement represented a political challenge to the state's credibility in asserting that existing welfare programs were appropriate responses to stagnation and unemployment. It was this legitimation function of the state that protected the privileged position of the corporate sector and consequently the strength of the system rested on its ability to coopt dissent, so "that conflict will be contained and minimized."[1]

It is clear from the summary of America and the New Era that the Student Movement was, in fact, preoccupied with theoretical problems, searching for ideas. . . . However, underdeveloped its themes, the evidence is here and cannot be swept away by those who simplify the posturings and ultimate ineffectiveness of its political action. America and the New Era outlined in implicit and undeveloped terms the nature of the governmental apparatus under advanced capitalism. It rooted the role of the state within the nature of the structural character of advanced industrial capitalism, identifying its two main economic

---

[1]Ibid., pg. 15.

functions as fiscal underwriter and social legiti-
mizer. The economic personality of the state is
determined by the contradictions inherent in this
stage of capitalist development.

> "it is clear that the old institutions
> and assumptions are not adequate to the
> technological revolution, and that
> central control, planning and integra-
> tion of the economy will have to occur.
> Insofar as the Administration has moved
> in this area, it has been in the direc-
> tion of supporting elitist, private,
> industry-wide 'planning' with the gov-
> ernment ratifying these plans as part of
> the corporate team."[1]

Building on the Port Huron Statement, America and
the New Era provided a more specific characterization of the role of the state under late capitalism and a better sense of the contemporary crisis
confronting the political economy. It outlined
the specific functions of the governmental apparatus in maintaining corporate hegemony over the
economy and linked economic hegemony to the
state's crucial role of legitimator and social
stabilizer. In short it identified the increased
interdependence of economic power on ideology -
even when that ideology characterized itself as a
non-ideology.

Another influential document that appeared around the time of America and the New Era
was entitled The Triple Revolution,[2] signed by
thrity-seven of the most prestigious social critics on the American scene, ranging from Michael
Harrington, Gunnar Myrdal, and Ben Seligman to

---

[1] Ibid., pg. 18.

[2] In fact one well-known member of SDS, Richard
Rothstein, has asserted that The Triple Revolution
paper had significant influence on the writing of
America and the New Era.

Linus Pauling, A. J. Muste, and Eric Fromm.[1] Its influence on SDS was direct and significant, for it not only shaped America and the New Era but it also led to the political analysis that projected the ERAP program which focused on the plight of the urban poor. SDS then looked to this social agency as the dynamic force that would begin a major movement for radical social change.

The Triple Revolution - the cybernetic age, the technology of arms, and the movement for human rights - focused on the cybernetic revolution and its relationship to the problem of income distribution. The essential problem facing the automated society was that of the allocation of demand in a society where income is generated from employment. The cybernetic revolution, the authors argued, produced a significant level of structural unemployment and consequently, effective demand would markedly fall short of productive potential.

"An adequate distribution of the potential abundance of goods and services will be achieved only when it is understood that the major economic problem is now how to increase production, but how to distribute the abundance that is the great potential of cybernation."[1]

The Triple Revolution argued that the governmental apparatus must institute planning mechanisms - under democratic organization - in order to manage the necessities forced by the automated era.

"We recognize that the drastic alternations in circumstances and in our way of life ushered in by cybernation and the economy of abundance will not be

---

[1]Donald Agger, et al., "The Triple Revolution," in Priscilla Long, op cit.

[2]Ibid., pg. 343.

completed overnight. Left to the ordinary forces of the market such change, however, will involve physical and psychological misery and perhaps political chaos."[1]

To SDS, The Triple Revolution and America and the New Era outlined the necessity for new political programs. These papers and others clearly projected the political expectation of "new insurgencies" among the poor, the black and the urban populations.[2] The crisis of the new technology coupled with the growing Civil Rights Movement pointed students away from the university and toward these new agencies of political mobilization. As Rothstein wrote:

"Equal opportunity was meaningless in a shrinking job market; the racial problem could not be dealt with unless obsolete economic arrangements were replaced."[3]

According to Sale and others, the growing estrangement from the life within the universities and the logic of these papers led SDS into the belief that the ghetto and the slum were the historically important areas[4] for political movement in the affluent society.[4]

The Question of Imperialism

The Port Huron Statement, America and the New Era, and The Triple Revolution were the

---

[1] Ibid., pg. 349.

[2] Particularly important was a paper presented by Ray Brown, Our Crisis Economy: The End of the Boom, cited in Sale, op cit., pg. 99.

[3] R. Rothstein, op cit., pg. 2.

[4] See particularly Sale, op cit., pgs. 95-102, and Unger, op cit. pgs. 54-60.

main documents in the Movement's attempt to define the political nature of modern American capitalism. None of these papers formally established a "name" for this new epoch of American capitalist development. The positions developed in these papers were essentially reformist in outlook. They were not intended as anti-capitalist critiques of American society. But in the years following their appearance the New Left had been moving away from reform towards a more damning characterization of the system. The struggle to "name the system" reflected this intellectual movement during the mid-sixties.

Nowhere was that developing critique more publicly identified than in two now famous anti-war speeches delivered during the spring and fall of 1965 by Paul Potter and Carl Ogelsby, respectively. Each was reprinted and well circulated.[1] The occasion was the first mass demonstration against the war in Vietnam on April 17, 1965. Paul Potter, then President of SDS, chose to speak on that "incredible war" in terms of the irrationality and hypocrisy of the Johnson administration's policy of plunder and destruction. Potter did not contain himself simply to admonishing responsible personalities, nor did he restrict himself to the domestic social costs of the military effort. What he did was to analyze American policy in Vietnam in terms of the overall "system" that produced such behavior, a systemic approach that was unconventional for that period of the peace movement.

Potter's remarks concluded with a challenge to his audience to "name" this system. He said:

---

[1]Paul Potter, "The Incredible War," in M. Teodori, op cit., pgs. 246-251 and Carl Ogelsby, "Trapped in a System," in M. Teodori, op cit., pgs. 182-188. The Ogelsby piece has appeared in several New Left readers, some cited in other parts of this manuscript.

"We must name that system. We must name it, describe it, analyze it, understand it and change it. For it is only when that system is changed and brought under control that there can be hope for stopping the forces that create war in Vietnam today or a murder in the South tomorrow. . .".[1]

These remarks signified the end of the reformist period of the Student Movement, for at this juncture, SDS programmatically recognized the American political system for what it was - a historically defined system of capitalist organization. It realized that the movement required a political critique of contemporary American capitalism and that no longer would fragmented analyses of parts of that system suffice as an explanation of the economic, political and social conditions affecting its generation.

Ogelsby's speech, delivered on October 27, 1965, attempted to identify the system that Potter indicted. Ogelsby began:

"Today I will try to name it - to suggest an analysis which to be quite frank, may disturb some of you - and to suggest what changing it may require of us."[2]

And to be sure Ogelsby upset his audience. At a time when the liberal civil rights alliance was coming unglued by the radical disenchantment with its reformist focus, particularly exemplified by the growing militancy of Student Non-violent Coordinating Committee (SNCC), Ogelsby put forth a direct indictment of American liberalism as the ideological framework for the justification of American cold war policy. Arguing that Vietnam

---

[1]M. Teodori, op cit., pg. 248.

[2]M. Teodori, op cit., pg. 182.

cannot simply be dismissed as the irrational policies of the contemporary incumbents in the White House, Pentagon, and State Department, Ogelsby reminded his audience of the ideological continuity surrounding American policy for some thirty-five years. He said:

"We must simply observe, and quite plainly say that this coalition, this blitzkrieg, and this demand for acquiescence are creatures, all of them, of a government that since 1932 has considered itself to be fundamentally liberal."[1]

After producing a litany of American interventions, disruptions, and covert operations into the affairs of foreign nations, Ogelsby asserted that the basic motivation for the American pursuit of empire was economic. He not only named the interventions but also the corporate relationships of the related American diplomats and peacemakers. In raising the then fresh spectre of the 1965 Dominican Republic affair in which 20,000 American marines were dispatched to keep the peace, Ogelsby indicated the corporate affiliations of the Johnson Administration policy makers.

"But how many also know that what was at stake was our new Caribbean Sugar Bowl? That this same neutral peacemaking [Ambassador Ellsworth] Bunker is a board member and stockowner of the National Sugar Refining Company, a firm his father founded in the good old days, and one which has a major interest in maintaining the status quo in the Dominican Republic? Or that the President's close personal friend and advisor, our new Supreme Court Justice Abe Fortas, has sat for the past 19 years on the board

---

[1]Ibid., pg. 182.

of the Sucrest Company, which imports black-strap molasses from the Dominican Republic? . . .".[1]

Finally the Student Movement had a name for the system. It was not simply the Establishment. It was now "corporate liberalism."

"This is the action of corporate liberalism. It performs for the corporate state a function quite like what the church once performed for the feudal state. It seeks to justify its burdens and protect it from change."[2]

An analysis that placed less weight on economic factors was introduced by Robert Wolfe in his article "American Imperialism and the Peace Movement," which appeared in the June 1966 issue of Studies on the Left.[3] Taking off on the Leninist model of imperialism, which he briefly described as the process whereby imperialism is an outgrowth of the surplus and investment glut in the domestic market which leads to the need for new markets abroad, Wolfe discounted the wholesale application of the Leninist framework to the American experience, particularly in Southeast Asia. He cited three basic reasons. First, United States foreign investment represented less than five percent of the total American capital investment, and surely this was not a critical proportion. Secondly, Wolfe noted that a serious disproportion existed between the actual pattern of American foreign policy and its foreign economic interests. While foreign investment significantly varied in absolute amounts between

---

[1] Ibid., pg. 185.

[2] Ibid., pg. 187.

[3] Robert Wolfe, "American Imperialism and the Peace Movement, Studies on the Left, Vol. 6 #3, May-June 1966.

the investments in the developed countries (particularly Canada and Western Europe) and that in the underdeveloped nations, American foreign policy seemed uniformly militant and intense in all parts of the world. No particular markets seemed to matter more than others, regardless of the strategic and economic promise of that market. Finally Wolfe argued that the Leninist model cannot account for the belligerence of the United States toward the "communist" world. Wolfe's characterization of the disparity between the reality of American foreign policy and the vitality of the Leninist model of imperialism was best summarized as follows:

> "In balance it seems to me that the Leninist thesis provides a necessary but not a sufficient explanation for the basic policies of American imperialism. American foreign policy is indeed designed to protect American investments abroad; the point is that it 'over protects' them, that it operates on a scale in a way which is all out of proportion to the magnitude of the interests at stake."[1]

Advocating a significantly different explanation of imperialism from the Leninist conceptualization, Wolfe set out to assemble a unique explanation whereby the imperialist character of American foreign policy is understood as a function of cold war military spending and its accompanying anti-communist ideology. Wolfe cites Paul Baran's The Political Economy of Growth in which Baran attempts to revive the Leninist framework by advocating that one must not simply consider the specific schedule of economic investments in exlaining international events. One must also factor in the entire structure of the military-industrial complex when making judgments about imperialist logic. Wolfe asserted that the

---

[1] Ibid., pg. 32.

American pursuit of the communist myth of a monolithic world-wide enemy resulted in an "over protection" of foreign investments whereby myth
becomes reality. Vietnam is the primary example
of this "over-reaction," where the myth of a
monolithic communist assault on Southeast Asia
resulted in the American deployment of a highly
inordinate proportion of its resources in an area
where American investment was insignificant by
comparison to other areas of the world.

In the same issue of Studies on the
Left, Aronson responded to the Wolfe thesis.[1]
Arguing that Wolfe overstated the role of myth,
Aronson asserted that capitalist competition with
communism is the real basis of American imperialism. American foreign policy retained a certain
uniformity because it was based on the protection
of the American foreign empire to the limits of
its real and potential borders.

Aronson disagreed with Wolfe on the
significance of American foreign investment.
While Wolfe noted that this activity amounted to
only five percent of total American capital investment, Aronson stated that these figures represented eleven percent of total profit. In addition Aronson asserted that the bulk of American
investment in the underdeveloped world was concentrated in raw materials, and consequently this
constituted a small but highly strategic proportion of American investment. Moreover, forty-five
corporations controlled approximately fifty percent of all foreign investment and to these inves-
tors, which as a group were highly influential
within the domestic market, foreign investment was
a significant factor in the overall conduct of
their operations. Finally, Aronson argued that
socialist revolution represents a universal threat
to the capitalist world beause it established an

---

[1]Ronald Aronson, "Socialism: The Sustaining
Menace," Studies on the Left, Vol. 6 #3, May-June
1966.

important political example to the remainder of the empire. To Aronson, American imperialism required uniform militance, for a hole anywhere in the dyke threatened the collapse of the entire fortress.

The significance of the Potter and Ogelsby speeches and the Wolfe and Aronson papers to the intellectual development of the Student Movement was the analysis of the imperialist component of modern capitalist political economy. Particularly important was their identification of the bureaucratic and ideological dimensions - as well as the economic factors - in the structure of imperialist foreign policy under advanced capitalism. Nevertheless this intellectual endeavor was short-lived within the Movement. By the late 1960's the Student Movement had abandoned its unique New Left character - at least intellectually - and had capitulated either to Old Left conceptions of imperialism from either a crude Leninist perspective or to an anarcho-moralistic vision.[1] Much more was written about imperialism within the movement, notably Carl Ogelsby's Containment and Change, however the theoretical understanding of imperialism never advanced beyond this initial challenge to the Leninist model or acceptance of it in some composit form.

With the last issue of Studies on the Left appearing in 1967, the dissemination of ideas was now channeled through pamphlets and miscellaneous conference papers and internal SDS docu-

---

[1]The former was the prevalent view of such Old Left student groups as the Progressive Labor Party's Worker-Student Alliance Caucus of SDS, the Socialist Workers Party's youth affiliate, the Young Socialist Alliance. The latter was characterized by the "white skin privilege" analysis of the Revolutionary Youth Movement I & II, the RYMI evolving into the Weatherman.

ments. The post-1967 period was characterized by the lack of theoretical consensus, focus and sophistication which, by the way, appears to be the main reason for the demise of Studies on the Left. Certainly several other factors were simultaneously at work - and the anti-ideological bias, the complexity of the questions before the movement, etc. - but the lack of a central journal certainly retarded the intellectual growth of the Student Movement. Other journals, such a Liberation and Radical America, did not fill the void created by the demise of Studies on the Left.[1] Neither was able to replace Studies' perceptive balance of theory and practice. Most likely the fall of Studies on the Left was due to the (1) growing debate over the primacy of either practice or theory, (2) the emergence of a new "generation" of leaders, less disposed to theoretical questions (as witnessed by SDS' Kewadin convention), and, (3) general disagreements over the political direction of the Movement. The theoretical focus shifted to more random forms of communication, particularly pamphlets and internal documents.

These events had a significant effect on the critique of modern capitalism which was evolving within movement circles since the appearance of The Port Huron Statement. It definitely stunted the growth of this critique. At the very least it delayed its intellectual maturity several years - several important years for the shape and direction of the Student Movement. However, an important paper that did continue to focus the movement's critique of modern capitalism was the previously cited piece by David Gilbert, et al., Consumption: Domestic Imperialism. This argument was presented in several versions with various contributors and under different titles in different places. The general argument appeared at

---

[1]Radical America was founded in 1967 by Paul Buhle and several other SDS people and after Studies on the Left folded. It was the only theoretical journal of the New Left.

a radical convention in 1967 as "The Port Authority Statement."[1] A somewhat altered version of their general theme was presented in SDS's newsletter, New Left Notes, under the title "Toward a Theory of Social Change in America."[2]

Gilbert outlined the basic characteristics of the contemporary oligopolistic form of capitalism: administered prices, market share as a measure of firm's success, new technology for lower costs instead of increased production, etc. However, Gilbert asserted that the major contradiction of advanced capitalism was the interplay between the corporate incentive for the introduction of advanced technology and the constant reality of the economy's tendency towards underconsumption. The tension between these polar forces is mediated by what Gilbert referred to as domestic and foreign imperialism:

> "In addition to limited redistribution of wealth and demand creation, modern capitalism deals with the problems of underconsumption through its policy of imperialism, both foreign and domestic."[3]

Foreign imperialism is the direct and indirect conquest of international markets. Domestic imperialism is the creation and extension of consumption-related activities, particularly the consumption, socialization and manipulation flowing from the extension of the cultural apparatus. The management of consumer demand is the domestic side of the 'imperialist' drive for new markets. An entire range of occupations connected with the state apparatus are specifically geared to the maintenance of the one dimensional world view.

---

[1] This conference was held at Princeton under the auspices of the Radical Education Project (REP).

[2] Gilbert, op cit., pg. 5

[3] Gilbert, Ibid., pg. 5.

Gilbert's paper was an attempt to integrate the cultural and psychological neo-Marxism of Marcuse with the new working class analysis then being introduced to the American movement. The strategical thrust of this analysis was the establishment of a revolutionary/radical identity for the Student Movement on its own terms. Students were defined as members of the new working class in the United States. The post-accumulative logic of the previously cited work by Martin Sklar, which appeared in Radical America in the spring, 1969, appears to build on the Gilbert piece. Technology has now eclipsed the question of scarcity and it has been able to produce a rising surplus with an ever-decreasing proportion of the workforce. This condition has given rise to the emergence of a superstructural apparatus which underwrites and ameliorates social conflict arising out of periodic economic crises and the maldistribution of wealth.

By 1969 and the appearance of the Sklar piece, the Student Movement had turned its focus from its New Left origins and began its masochistic discovery of the most crude interpretations of the Leninist and anarchist traditions. The intellectual advancement of the American Marxism and neo-Marxism fell to groups outside the leadership of the popular movements. The critique of modern capitalism within the movement never reached the stage of theoretical perspective but rather rested with the popular concept of corporate liberalism. It never attained the level of theoretical sophistication that would allow it to perform the much-needed role of strategic prescription. Instead it lay in abeyance, destined to serve as a disjointed indictment of the self-serving foreign policy with vague roots in the domestic social order.

The New Left Student Movement was primarily concerned with its social practice. Consequently one would expect its most developed intellectual endeavor would have been concerned with those issues surrounding strategy and tactics. And in fact the most involved aspect of the Student Movement's political analysis was its prolonged search for an agency for social change. Its most intense intellectual experience was its political exploration of several social groupings. First, it identified with the intelligentsia, then deserting the campus for the Southern and Northern huddles of the poor, only to return to the "industrialized" campus as the training center of the new working class, and finally the recapitulation to the old working class and/or the 'third world.'

Born in an age of the "end of ideology" the Student Movement was burdened with the dual task of first restoring the legitimacy of political reflection and action, and then re-examining the political potential of the intellectual tradition of the American radical heritage. Under these conditions there was no consensus on the question of agency nor was there any understood political identity for the movement itself. In many ways the search for agency was itself the search for a political self-identity by the Student Movement. So, beginning with its liberal reformist posture, the Student Movement initially defined itself as a social catalyst for other groups - most particularly the dominant institutions of the "progressive" heritage. As it moved toward the development of its programs, especially SDS's ERAP organizing of the Northern white poor, the movement sought to identify with other agencies. With the collapse of these programs and the failure to maintain an alliance with the Civil Rights Movement in a period of rising Black nationalism, the "outcast" Student Movement returned to its campus base. Finally the limitations of a narrow student base became obvious in the face of a sustained imperialist war policy, and the Student Movement was forced once again to the question of agency. Only this time, the post-1968 period of the movement sought radical social change and not merely mass resistance or liberal reform. The movement necessarily had to confront the only developed critique of capitalism. And so Marx and the question of class. But here the anti-ideological bias would drive the movement toward the most crude adaption of what Mills had previously referred to as "vulgarized marxism." Clearly the disjunction between theory and practice was most obvious during that period. Instead of the movement's unification with the New Left Idea and the wholesale popularization of a neo-marxist perspective, the movement fell back upon what Marx would have characterized as "all the old crap."

The Political Role of Intellectuals

The Port Huron Statement was written by and for a student audience. The document is concerned with the political potential of students as a distinct social catalyst for significant political change. The thrust of the document was the exhortation of the young intelligentsia to announce their co-belligerency with the poor, the black, and the third world in the causes of peace and equality. There was no sense of students and intellectuals as the main body of a new class, or in any other way as a strategically superior social formation. Rather The Port Huron Statement morally cajoles the young intelligentsia to respond to the contemporary state of affairs. They are to join forces with and form alliances among the other progressive liberal forces on the American scene.

Even as late as 1964, this voluntaristic perspective on the political role of the intellectual was a significant viewpoint. Paul Potter, President of SDS, wrote at that time:

"But there is a new understanding, gained through direct participation in social movements, that power is something that can be created, that it can

182

be generated at the base of the social structure; and the intellectual can obtain power by involving himself in the emerging centers of power in society: the civil rights movement, the peace movement, the discussion of economic issues."[1]

The political role of the intellectual was not understood in any significant sense as a distinct political group. The same theme was struck in an important address given by Staughton Lynd to the New University Conference (NUC) in March, 1968. The university and the intellectual were not themselves important political artifacts because they are perceived by Lynd as "powerless." They gain power in their voluntary association with other groups. "To do this, we ourselves must have a foot solidly off the campus."[2]

This position displays a fundamental incoherence between the Student Movement and the New Left Idea. New Left theory definitely outlined the critical role played by the cultural apparatus in the reproduction of a hegemonic and repressive social environment. This intensified ideological domination represented a qualitative change in cultural hegemony, characterized by new forms of social control. The cultural dimension dramatically affected the expectations and overall behavior pattern of the individual, as well as his structure of personality. The Student Movement's position ignored the critical role played by the intellectuals in the reproduction of a system supportive social consciousness. Instead of identifying their political importance, the movement underestimated their significance for late

---

[1] Paul Potter, ".The Intellectual and Social Change" in Cohen and Hale, op cit., pg. 20.

[2] Staughton Lynd, "The Responsibility of Intellectuals," reprinted in Mitchell Goodman, ed., The Movement Toward a New America, (Philadelphia: Pilgrim Press, 1970).

capitalism, demeaned their strategic location and downplayed their political value.

The Student Movement never did reverse its assumption on the political role of intellectuals. Although the New Left perspective recognized the political existence of intellectuals, it never outlined an exhaustive analysis that elevated intellectuals to an independent strategic force. Rather they were lumped into the vague category of the "new class and were not perceived as an autonomous political grouping to be organized for their respective political function in the mode of consciousness production and maintenance. Alternatively, the "poor" and the "new working class" were not identified as agencies for change in such a cavalier style. Their strategic positioning was based on more sophisticated reasoning.

The Poor As Agency for Change

Two days following the Civil Rights Movement's 1963 March on Washington, Students for a Democratic Society initiated its Economic Research and Action Program (ERAP). Intellectually founded on the "new insurgencies" arguments of both The Triple Revolution paper and the second major SDS statement, America and the New Era, ERAP was a series of geographically dispersed organizing projects set in poor white Northern communities. In June 1963 there were ten project sites - Baltimore, Boston, Chester, Pa., Chicago, Cleveland, Hazard, Ky., Lousiville, Newark, Philadelphia, and Trenton. Somehow SDS had raised $20,000 as seed money to carry these programs through the summer of 1963. By the fall 1964 ERAP was reduced to four stable projects: Baltimore, Chicago, Cleveland and Newark. By 1967 only Newark and Chicago remained. The Newark project died in the wake of the 1967 ghetto riots and the Chicago site gradually withered away.

Stimulated by the political barbs of the more militant sections of the Civil Rights Movement, SDS founded ERAP in order to provide a white base of support for Southern poor Blacks.[1] The task of organizing against racism in the South was somewhat stabilized after the 1963 March on Washington. What remained a problem for the Civil Rights Movement was the maintenance of growth of a politically potent white alliance. ERAP was, in part, a response to this need. However, ERAP was also an attempt to build a "class" wide movement of the poor and unemployed as a prelude to a national movement for radical social change.

The ERAP program had three main goals.[2] It was hoped that northern community organizing among the poor and unemployed would act as a catalyst for the liberal forces within the American polity. ERAP assumed that liberals were politically focused on the cold war logic of the warfare state instead of the needed progressive social programs required to ameliorate the conditions of racism and poverty. Secondly, ERAP was intended to produce actual achievements in local political and social reform particularly in the area of social services. It was hoped that local movements would force the national political leadership to reassess the current proportion of domestic resources allocated to defense related activity at the expense of social welfare programs. Finally, ERAP was intended to counter the white backlash to the Civil Rights Movement by building an interracial movement of the poor.

---

[1] For instance, see The Vine City Project, "The Vine City Project Paper on 'Whites in the Movement'", in Cohen and Hale, ed., op cit., pgs. 97-108. The Vine City Project was a community organizing group affiliated with the Student Nonviolent Coordinating Committee (SNCC). This paper proceeded SNCC's formal adoption of black nationalism.

[2] Both K. Sale, op cit., and R. Rothstein, op cit. concur on these three goals basing their interpretations on documents, interviews and in Rothstein's case, personal history.

The first two goals were directly advocated in America and the New Era. The general political malaise which dominated liberal circles was described in specific terms throughout that document.

"American leaders are presently engaged in a politics of adjustment, affecting the conduct of government, industry, the military and all other social institutions. This politics represents an attempt to manage social conflict and adjust in minimal ways to the forces loose in the world."[1]

And later on the authors asserted that, ". . . Liberalism has adopted a neutral managerial role."[2] The means for the enactment of liberal program was, ". . . the organization of disenfranchised groups for the effective exercise of their political power. . .".[3]

The third goal, the building of a national movement of the poor and disenfranchised, was embodied in a number of position papers and internal documents of SDS. A continuous dialogue on the political potential of the poor was carried on in movement circles during the mid-sixties. The best known and most influential of these was a paper written by Tom Hayden and Carl Wittman entitled An Interracial Movement of the Poor?, presented as a contribution to the founding of ERAP.[4]

Hayden and Wittman presented a lucid analysis of the political realities surrounding

---

[1]SDS, op cit., pg. 2.

[2]Ibid., pg. 24.

[3]Ibid., pg. 24.

[4]See K. Sale, Op cit., pg. 105

the white northern poor and the exigencies confronting the organizing effort required to reach this constituency. Their paper was not so much a polemic on "why the poor as agency for change" as it was an assessment of "how to organize the poor for social change." The authors were looking toward an interracial movement, ". . . because a program based primarily on race will not improve the terrible social conditions which provide the impetus for the movement."[1] The method of achieving an integrated movement lay in the assertion of, "demands for political and economic changes of substantial benefit to the Negro and white poor." Such issues were better housing, schools, full employment, etc. At the time this paper was written the Civil Rights Movement was exclusively concerned with the winning of legal rights for Blacks and the elimination of the formal areas of racial discrimination. Its focus was devoid of any materialist viewpoint.

The authors asserted that "Negroes, Puerto Ricans, Mexicans and Indians" shared a basic sense of exploitation and estrangement. However, in the northern urban areas, eastern and southern European ethnic groups resting at the bottom of class stratification perceived these other minority groups as a challenge to their anxious economic condition. The authors argued that without organizing a movement of the poor around unemployment and automation, any chance for an alliance between Negroes and European ethnics would be lost and a strong backlash to the Civil Rights Movement would ensue. In commenting on the SDS Chicago based project, Jobs or Income Now (JOIN), Hayden and Wittman specifically asserted the political necessity of these issues for an interracial movement.

---

[1]Tom Hayden and Carl Wittman, "An Interracial Movement of the Poor?" reprinted in Cohen and Hale, ed., op cit., pg. 177.

"More surprisingly the whites, though fewer in number, express a real interest in becoming involved in JOIN, and most see racism as a diversionary issue. The advantage of initiating a project with the explicit intention of building interracial unity around the jobs issue are quite obvious: The movement is immediately political, the service-centered aspects of the project do not become more consuming than issues and programs, etc."[1]

The traditional agency for change - the working class - was identified by Hayden and Wittman as ". . . reactionary people, many trying to consolidate the achievements made during the generations since their families immigrated here."[2] Caught in the contradiction between an impending economic collapse (as outlined by America and the New Era) and their relatively privileged position stemming from organized labor's ties to the corporate world and tradi-tional political institutions, the working class was likely to resist an alliance with the poor and black of the Civil Rights Movement. In general, An Interracial Movement of the Poor? implies that the political potential of the working class has been eclipsed by their economic and political assimilation in the fabric of contemporary American capitalism. Although this condition is not a permanent one, the authors argued that this group seems to be foreclosed from playing a major role for significant social change in the near future. The poor, on the other hand, were much more conscious of their relative disadvantages and more likely to act on their feelings of political disenfranchisement and social isolation. Hayden and Wittman asserted that the political potential of the poor was superior to the working class and

---

[1] Ibid., pg. 199.

[2] Ibid., pg. 200.

a more viable catalyst for the building of a radical political movement that seeks:

> ". . . democratic participation in a society with a publicly-controlled and planned economy, which guarantees political freedom, economic and physical security, abundant education, and incentives for wide cultural variety."[1]

As the ERAP program developed, the controversy over the correctness of SDS's focus on the poor intensified significantly. Todd Gitlin, a former president of SDS, wrote a popular position paper surveying the early experience of ERAP. In his essay, The Radical Potential of the Poor, Gitlin asserted that the poor:

> ". . . exhibit a potential for movement - for understanding their situation, breaking loose, and committing themselves to a radical alternative."[2]

Arguing that the 'underclass' has its most 'abrasive' experience with the dominant vested interests of American society, "less at the point of production than outside it," Gitlin proclaimed that the poor gain a radical political consciousness through their varied confrontations with the political elite in several policy areas and ultimately begin to interconnect these experiences so as to construct a more complete understanding of the hierarchical composition of American politics. By organizing the poor around local reform issues - such as housing, employment and education - the questions of the access to power, the legitimacy of authority and the control over public policy

---

[1] Ibid., pg. 211.

[2] Todd Gitlin, "The Radical Potential of the Poor," reprinted in Mathew Stolz, The Politics of the New Left (Beverly Hills: Glencoe Press, 1971), pg. 111.

are necessarily raised. The corporate and hierarchical bias of the system become self-evident. The community unions and other local organizing projects find and must sustain a "culture of resistance" among the poor.

The political potential of the poor lies in their ability to develop a radical political consciousness by virtue of their position in society and the social experience that it offers slum residents. The traditional working class does not share this experience, according to Gitlin.

"Propped by a unifying ideology of free enterprise, nationalism, and law and order, the class-consciousness of the well fed worker, blue or white collar, is limited by his relative prosperity; that of the slum dweller, by his contacts with city bureaucracies and the shifting middle class. But the poor are probably still better equipped to understand - and find 'new' ways of understanding - the class structure of American society than are most organized workers."[1]

Drawing from an article written by Norman Fruchter and Robert Kramer that appeared in Studies on the Left, Gitlin argues that to deny the possibility of these secondary forms of exploitation as opposed to the primary form of class exploitation would be to assert an iron law of consciousness.[2]

In a response to the ERAP's community organizing approach Ronald Aronson outlined the criticism of ERAP within the New Student Left.

---

[1] Ibid., pg. 122.

[2] See Norman Fruchter and Robert Kramer, "An Approach to Community Organizing," Studies on the Left, Vol. 6 #2, March-April 1966.

Writing about the incoherence of social theory and movement experience, Aronson argued that the radical potential of the poor was indeed a limited one. Because of their economic marginality and need for immediate reform the poor are unlikely to call into question the very legitimacy of the system. With the poor as agency for change, the political potential of the movement is itself limited.

> "But because of its built in limits, a movement of the poor must continue to drift between its demands for reform and its sense of total opposition to the system, becoming neither strictly reformist nor fully radical."[1]

Sounding a similar political argument, Kimberly Moody asserted that, historically, those in the worst economic straits has never been the social agencies of structural change. Rather it has been those forces which are newly exploited - those on a downward direction of the social hierarchy - that have experienced the structural contradictions and ideological myths of the prevailing social order which have been organized into movements for fundamental political and economic reorganization.[2] Finally, Eugene Genovese capsulized the growing criticism of the community organizing focus of SDS when in a 1966 article appearing in the newsweekly, The Guardian, he wrote:

> "No matter how effective or promising or romantically appealing work in the ghettos may be, the main task remains to win the American masses, which are

---

[1]Ronald Aronson, "The Movement and Its Critics," Studies on the Left, Vol. 6 #1, January-February 1966, pg. 8.

[2]Kimberly Moody, "Can the Poor Be Organized?", in Cohen and Hale, op cit., pgs. 153-159

increasingly 'middle class' in their outlook and character."[1]

The debate over the poor as social agency continued within the inner circles of the Movement until the mid-sixties when in the face of an expanding economy instead of a slumping one, and a growing war of colonialist intervention and its anti-war movement antithesis, the ERAP program collapsed. The community organizing projects failed to build an interracial movement of the poor because of unexpected economic growth instead of stagnation, as well as the failure of the subjective forces to organize around the reformist consciousness and materialist aspirations of the underclass. In a real sense, the ERAP organizers were unable to grasp the assimilationist desires of the white urban poor, who although aware of the structural inequalities of the contemporary American order, simply sought their "piece of pie." Although the withering away of ERAP by 1967 foreclosed the poor as agency to the Student Movement, it allowed the question of class consciousness - and more particularly "false consciousness" - to surface within the intellectual arenas of the Movement. And the question of consciousness brought with it the necessity for some understanding of the political economic and cultural dynamics surrounding late capitalism.

The New Working Class

From 1966 to 1968 the new working class analysis surfaced within the Student Movement. At the SDS national convention in August 1966, Carl Davidson presented a position paper entitled, Toward a Student Syndicalist Movement, or University Reform Revisited. The thrust of Davidson's remarks was the identification of the corporate

---

[1]Eugene Genovese, "Genovese Looks at the American Left - New and Old," The Guardian, February 1966, pg. 7.

bonds of the contemporary American university system. Establishing the link between corporate liberalism and the American university, Davidson asserted that the political function of modern higher education was the training of future corporate elites and the mass of educated laborers who would fill crucial positions within the corporate institutional fabric.

"Our education institutions 'are' corporations and knowledge factories. What we have failed to see in the past is how absolutely vital these factories are to the corporate liberal state."[1]

Although the "knowledge factories" produce knowledge, their main commodity is the knowledgeable." The main output of the modern university, according to Davidson, was the continuous flow of educated labor into middle management positions in the corporate hierarchy.

"As integral parts of the knowledge factory system, we are both the exploiters and the exploited. As both the managers and the managed, we produce and become the most vital product of corporate liberalism: bureaucratic man."[2]

Davidson's paper did not specifically identify the modern mass-university student as a member of the new working class. His analysis was the forerunner of a more fully developed thesis that developed over the following two years. However, the impact of his presentation on the

---

[1]Carl Davidson, "Toward a Student Syndicalist Movement, or University Reform Revisited," reprinted in I Wallerstein and P. Starr, ed., op cit., Vol. II, pg. 99.

[2]Ibid., pg. 100.

SDS delegates was a significant factor in his election to the post of vice-president of SDS.[1]

In the winter and spring of 1967 the new working class label was initially introduced to the Student Movement. In February 1967 Greg Calvert, national secretary of SDS, delivered a speech at a Princeton Conference of SDS which was reprinted under the title, <u>In White America: Radical Consciousness and Social Change</u>.[2] Arguing that only "a truly radical, an authentically revolutionary movement for change" will correct the social ills of American society, Calvert identified the major problem confronting the radical forces as the "search for constituency, for an agent of social transformation, for the 'revolutionary class.'"

Defining revolutionary movement as "freedom struggles born out of perception of the contradictions between human potentiality and oppressive actuality"[3], Calvert wrote that revolutionary consciousness becomes the glue between movement and ideas, between actuality and potentiality.

> "No individual, no group, no class is genuinely engaged in a revolutionary movement unless their struggle is a struggle for their own liberation."[4]

---

[1] James O'Brien argues this point in his history of the American New Left, <u>A History of the American New Left</u>, 1960-1968 (Boston: New England Free Press).

[2] Greg Calvert, "In White America: Radical Consciousness and Social Change," reprinted in M. Teodori, <u>op</u> <u>cit</u>., pgs. 412-18.

[3] <u>Ibid</u>., pg. 413.

[4] <u>Ibid</u>., pg. 414.

Guilt over the plight of the poor, minority groups, or the third world will not fuel the necessary developments in consciousness and political activity in the building of a revolutionary movement in contemporary America.

The problem facing the New Left, according to Calvert, was one of the failure to recognize the lack of freedom. This is a problem of false consciousness, ". . . the failure to perceive one's situation in terms of oppressive (class) relationships."[1] New radicals failed to understand that their feelings of alienation and estrangement with modern capitalist America "could be understood in terms of a fundamental and critical analysis of American corporate-liberal capitalism." Radicals must understand that the widespread feelings of alienation among the young are occurring during a period of widespread prosperity and consumption. Material satisfaction alone cannot preclude the development of radical consciousness in the midst of an irrational social order. Aren't there other experiences besides material satisfaction which can radicalize human beings?

> "It is perhaps the failure of the old left to arrive at a satisfactory answer to that question which was responsible for its fervent attachment to the concept of the inevitability of the collapse of capitalism. . ."[2]

To Calvert the "new working class" thesis provided a powerful analytic concept for understanding the workings of modern technological society and the rise of the contemporary student revolt. It offered a new identity to the Student Movement. It shattered the myth of the middle class by asserting the working class base of

---

[1] _Ibid._, pg. 415.

[2] _Ibid._, pg. 416.

educated labor in a bureaucratic and technocratic world. It also identified the role of students as trainees and apprentices for the new work force, presently housed in universities until they will man the machinery of corporate capitalism. Students then are part of the very agency they need to be organizing for social change. Concentration on other agencies by students - such as the poor - are misplaced efforts for any long run effort at structural change. It is within the professional strata that false consciousness is wearing away - in the spheres of the social workers, teachers, etc. The new working class will recognize its oppression and link itself to other oppressed groups not out of guilt but because of the need for their own liberation.

Carl Davidson added his voice to the call for the development of political consciousness in an SDS pamphlet published in 1968, updating his original analysis outlined in Toward a Student Syndicalist Movement, called The New Radicals and the Multiversity. Davidson clearly states that the goal of the student power movement is not simply the liberalization of the university but rather the

> ". . . development of a radical political consciousness among those students who later hold jobs in strategic sectors of the political economy."[1]

Identifying the university as a major part of the cultural apparatus, Davidson argued that modern higher education performed the crucial tasks of socializing the new working class to the dominant values of corporate America as well as familiarizing them with some of the important characteristics of modern large-scale industry. Hierarchy, the division of labor and specializa-

---

[1]Carl Davidson, "The New Radicals and the Multiversity," reprinted in M. Teodori, op cit., pg. 324.

ation were easily transmitted in the modern university by the use of grades and class rankings. Students learn to be alienated - or expect to maintain this sense of estrangement - from the product of their work and the work process itself. What they learn, how they learn it and why are all determined by forces over which they have no control. Their actual education is not beyond the "consumption and distribution of data and technique."

The new working class analysis put forth in the Student Movement, most prolifically by Davidson and Calvert, was an attempt at coherence between the New Left Idea and the practice of the Movement. It casually addressed the question of consciousness, late capitalism and agency. But the point is that it did address them, however nonchalantly and imprecisely. For a moment - between 1966-1968 in the American experience - the Idea and the Movement reached something approaching ideological juncture. The failure of the merger of thought and action to maintain itself and grow with events was an involved problem reserved for discussion in the following section of this manuscript. However it is safe to say that one element in that failure was the undeveloped character of the movement's analysis, particularly on the relationship between the breakdown of false consciousness within the new working class and the reaction to it by the old working class. In general the new working class while providing a historic identity for students, failed to extend the analysis of late capitalism beyond this constituency. The post-Chicago events following the 1968 Democratic Convention firmly established revolutionary and strategy as the popular focus of the Movement but in part the undeveloped character of the neo-capitalist and new working class analyses contributed to the Movement's turn back to other agencies, particularly minority groups and the third world. Some students drifted back to the old working class and the crude marxism of the Progressive Labor Party and its Worker-Student Alliance Caucus within SDS. Given the fragility of the New Left Idea and its popular adaption

within the Student Movement, the post-1968 era was
marked by either wholesale adaptions of the orthodox Marxist-Leninist model of revolution or the
barren adventurism of the third world worship
projected by what would ultimately become the
Revolutionary Youth Movement I (Weatherman).

Conclusion

The New Left Student Movement ceased functioning as a New Left movement in the post-Chicago
period. In the rush to find a theorectical
vehicle for revolutionary change the Student
Movement returned to the vanguarditis of the Old
Left Leninist heritage. In part this was due to
the theoretical poverty of American radicalism
which the New Left inherited. It was also a
function of the undeveloped character of the New
Left Idea and the popular interpretations of it
within the Student Movement.

The intellectual contribution of the Movement
was its focus on the cultural prerequisites for
political stability under modern capitalism. The
Student Movement popularized C. Wright Mill's
dichotomy between "public issues and private
troubles." It identified the political role of
the cultural apparatus and in casual ways it
allowed the question of false consciousness to
surface in the public arena. The Movement was
able to link the questions of consciousness and
agency to some general critique of the corporate
bias of the modern state under late capitalism.
In short, the Student Movement provided the New
Left Idea with a public profile in spite of the
fact that its behavior provided public mispercep-
tion of the basic foundations of the New Left
Idea.

Lacking anything approaching a sophisticated
understanding of the historical process and the
dynamics of political economy, the Student Movement was unable to sustain coherence with the New
Left Idea for any significant period of time.
Nonetheless the Movement represented an important

step forward in the development of an American neo-marxist praxis because of its negation of the determinist heritage of the American Old Left and the refocusing of radical political thought on the unique character of advanced capitalism and its critical reliance on the cultural dimension of economic stability and social control. The collapse of the Student Movement shortly after the spring of the Cambodian invasion and the killings at Kent State were as much a function of the non-"new left" character of the movment at that time as they were a political consequence of its undeveloped New Left ideology and current practice. The political potential of the New Left Idea in the American context is the central concern of the final section of this manuscript.

PART THREE:

THE NEW LEFT AND MARXIST THEORY

The New Left Idea and the intellectual dimension of the contemporary American Student Movement
were distinct entities which share a mutual heritage. Yet a significant portion of the evaluative
literature - critical or sympathetic - on the New
Left treats the Student and New Left Movements as
identical. In the main, the literature critical
of the New Left either fails to assemble a comprehensive structure of its ideas or it avoids deal-
ing with the validity of the New Left's concept of
cultural hegemony and everyday life. Assailing
the utopian character of the New Left Idea and
condemning the experiential style of its political
practice, the critics fail to encounter its intellectual focus - the political role of contemporary
culture - and therefore they avoid the question of
social consciousness under capitalism. In side-
stepping the question of consciousness and its
relationship to the cultural composition of
capitalism, these critics of the New Left present
an incomplete evaluation of the historical importance of this movement, for the central paradox
confronting American marxism and neo-marxism is
its inability to explain capitalism's self-
rationalizing mechanisms and its concurrent containment of social consciousness. To condemn the
New Left without evaluating its position on this
central question, is to condemn one's analysis as
fragmented and disjointed. For American marxism
to preserve its essential intellectual force it
must, above all, be able to explain the configuration of modern American capitalism and the reasons
for its popular base. Without a theoretical
explanation of the success of capitalism, marxism
becomes an obscure and dated school of philosophical inquiry.

On the other hand the literature sympathetic
to the New Left omits a critique of the theoretical limitations of the New Left Idea. Specifically, it has been neglectful in outlining the shortcomings of the Freudian naturalism basic to the

composition of the New Left's cultural analysis. Quick to establish the linkage between the sociological and psychological prerequisites of the modern capitalist order, the sympathetic work on the New Left has not carefully treated the "instinctual" assumptions in its cultural critique which eliminated the concept of "class" as a significant category of modern industrial society. The loss of "class" was a significant failure of the New Left Idea and the continuation of the "instinctual" bias by those sympathetic to New Left Idea does not contribute to the development of the Idea but rather points to the non-dialectic nature of its analysis.

Both the negative and positive reviews of the New Left Idea fall into these incomplete categories. Each has failed to describe and evaluate the New Left Idea in a historically significant manner; that is to say, the literature on the New Left omits (1) a comprehensive presentation of the theoretical heritage and intellectual foundation of the New Left, (2) an assessment of the logical consistency of its political analysis, (3) any attempt at identifying the juncture of its theory and practice and (4) any projection of its heuristic value. They either do not confront the importance of the question of cultural hegemony or they neglect any serious questioning of its neo-Freudian character. In this section of the manuscript, the best of the evaluative literature on the New Left will be discussed, the Idea itself will be reviewed, and an attempt will be made to go beyond the New Left in the outline of several steps in the direction of a new _praxis_.

Critical Reviews of the New Left Idea

Perhaps the most developed and comprehensive critical evaluation of the New Left Idea is presented in Peter Clecak's Radical Paradoxes: Dilemmas of the American Left, 1945-1970.[1] Clecak

---

[1]Peter Clecak, _op_ _cit_.

goes well beyond any of the popular literature in examining the make-up of the New Left Idea, but nevertheless his work suffers from the same theoretical flaw that plagues all of the Old Left critiques of the New Left. He avoids the question of contemporary social consciousness and its relationship to the cultural mechanisms of modern capitalism. He avoids any involved analysis of the political significance of the hegemonic role played by the cultural dimension in the everyday life patterns of modern society.

To Clecak the fundamental paradox confronting the American Left is the enigma of its own political ineffectiveness.

"Viewed from every serious radical perspective, the historical situation itself has enforced the paradox of powerlessness on Leftists of every ideological cast."[1]

Placed among the historically obscure, the Left searches for its own identity among the complexity of modern industrial society. To Clecak the "plain marxists," Mills, Marcuse, Baran and Sweezy, sought to unravel the central political contradictions of advanced capitalism and to assess the possibility of radical social change. Accordingly the theoreticians of the New Left Idea broke from the traditional categories of radical thinking imposed on them by the Old Left heritage. But here is where Clecak believes their fundamental contradiction arises.

"Whereas democratic socialists typically attenuated the dilemmas by insisting upon the unity of socialism and democracy, 'plain Marxists' came to insist on the unity of socialism (or more precise-

---

[1]Ibid., pg. 6.

203

ly communism) and community. This
difference proved to be decisive."[1]

To Clecak the New Left is characterized by a constant utopian seam which led it to neglect
present-day probabilities in favor of future
possibilities.

"The basic pattern thus exhibits a
certain symmetry. Taken together, plain
Marxists of the postwar period reversed
older priorities of social change in
order to save their long-range moral and
social visions; they moved away from
awkward characterizations of radical
paradoxes within history toward projected resolutions beyond history, exchanging the broken promises of socialism for
illusions of communism."[2]

The New Left Idea was bound to a dialectic of liberation where the need for community and the abolition of exploitation and alienation become the
central focus of politics. In Clecak's analysis:

"Instead of insisting on a democratic
socialism whose arrival seemed endlessly
delayed, they (The New Left theorits,
the 'plain marxists') made more ambi-
tious utopian claims on the historical
present, confusing the struggle for
democracy with the abolition of alienation."[3]

---

[1]Ibid., pg. 20. Clecak is critical of the democratic socialists' insistence on parliamentary
means in achieving revolutionary goals, while he
is equally frustrated with the utopian ends of the
New Left.

[2]Ibid., pgs. 29-30.

[3]Ibid., pg. 30.

The foundation of Clecak's analysis became apparent in his commentary on Marcuse, the New Left and his assessment of the future of socialism. Characterizing Marcuse as a "cultural astronomer" Clecak attempts to foreclose a good deal of Marcuse's political analysis by limiting his critique to Marcuse's aesthetics. Clecak relegates the bulk of critical theory to this abbreviated analytic space.

"Critical theory is essentially a double optic with two main analytic dimensions - a version of the present and a vision of the future. Together, these two lenses bring a third, implicit political dimension into obscure and changing focus."[1]

Clecak argues that this "double optic" precludes an historical analysis from emerging within Marcuse's work.

"Refusing to abandon the Communist vision as the supreme goal of history, he fails to offer convincing assessments of prospects for various modes of socialism around the world. Like others who hold to the dialectic of liberation, Marcuse cannot estimate the slim historical and political chances of doing away with capitalist forms of exploitation and establishing democratic norms and institutions in socialist societies."[2]

Clecak's characterization of Marcuse is extreme and unfair. If Marcuse's work would be described as any one thing, clearly that would be as an analysis of contemporary social consciousness and the forms of mass manipulation inherent in the political and cultural design of advanced

---

[1]Ibid., pg. 183.

[2]Ibid., pg. 227.

industrial society. What is <u>One Dimensional Man</u> if not a treatise on the existence of false consciousness and the consequent limitations on modern day political practice for any significant alteration of the contemporary configuration of power? Surely it is a pessimistic analysis of the roots of modern power politics within advanced societies and the possibility of political change in the foreseeable future. If anything, Marcuse's work stands as <u>precisely</u> an estimation of the 'historically possible' in the twentieth century. His analysis may be error-prone, but Clecak confounds our understanding of it by condemning Marcuse for his utopian wanderings and aesthetic features.

The fundamental flaw of <u>Radical Paradoxes</u> is its failure to evaluate the "plain marxists" on their own terrain. Clecak avoids any discussion of the legitimacy of the theoretical focus of the New Left Idea - cultural hegemony and contemporary consciousness. He neglects to explain how he thinks social consciousness is formed and developed under advanced capitalism. He omits any discussion of what kind of socialist politics would heighten or retard consciousness. The paradox of <u>Radical Paradoxes</u> is Clecak's failure to take on the legitimacy of the cultural question.

In his assessment of the future of socialism Clecak makes clear his refusal to link the "personal and the political."

"In between [life and death under democratic socialism], the painful search for personal coherence and meaning, the evanescence of success and tragedy of individual failure, and the fragile, transient character of personal relationships will presist, ensuring a wide range of possibilities for individual happiness and misery."[1]

---

[1]<u>Ibid</u>., pg. 285

Clecak argues that the nature and intensity of personal experience will be altered by the social context of democratic socialism. But somehow the reader is left with the distinct impression that it is at the point of the new society that a new social consciousness, and the link of personal and political experience, will emerge. Clecak does not discuss the process of consciousness development under capitalism and thereby avoids the question of hegemony. He condemns his analysis to the paradoxical categories of the Old Left's social democratic heritage.

The writings of Christopher Lasch are similarly characterized by a lack of any intellectual resolution of the legitimacy of the cultural focus of the New Left Idea. Lasch is somewhat more insightful than Clecak in that he eventually recognizes the correctness of the cultural question but he omits any evaluation of the theoretical efforts of Mills and Marcuse. Lasch admits that ideology and culture are the important analytic categories for the construction of any contemporary radical social theory.

In The Agony of the American Left, Lasch confined his assessment of the New Left to the simple practical politics of its movements, never venturing into the areas of its implicit and explicit intellectual foundations.

"The New Left's cheif contribution to American politics, so far, is that together with the war in Vietnam, it has moved many liberals several degrees leftward."[1]

To Lasch the hope of this movement laid on its ability

". . . to generate analysis and plans for action in which people of varying

---

[1]Christopher Lasch, op cit., pg. 188.

commitment to radicalism can take part, while at the same time it must insist that the best hope of creating a decent society in the United States is to evolve a socialism appropriate to American conditions."[1]

In perhaps his most involved analysis of the New Left Idea, Lasch began to focus on the question of contemporary culture in his essay, "Is Revolution Obsolete?", which appeared in final form in a collection of essays published in 1973 under the title, The World of Nations.[2] Here he does review some of the intellectual underpinnings of the New Left but he criticized the New Left for confusing personal liberation and personal authenticity "with the search for cultural alternatives to capitalism." To Lasch the New Left associated personal liberation with freedom from authority and the work ethic. Lasch believes that this is a fundamental intellectual error because it redirected the political focus onto leisure and the non-work dimension of culture life.

> "Contrary to a widespread cliche of popular sociology, 'the challenge of leisure' is not the most important issue in advanced society. The most important issue remains work - the loss of autonomy on the job, the collapse of high standards of workmanship, the pervasive demoralization that results from the mass production of goods that are widely recognized as intrinsically worthless by those who produce them, and the general crisis of culture historically oriented around the dignity of labor."[3]

---

[1] Ibid., pg. 201.

[2] Christopher Lasch, The World of Nations (New York: Vintage, 1974).

[3] Christopher Lasch, "Is Revolution Obsolete," Ibid., pg. 115.

To Lasch the manner in which the Student Movement projected the question of political culture was directly responsible for the isolation of that movement from a popular base. By portraying the cultrual domain as monolithic and bourgeois at its core, the Student Movement was unable to confront the disorder and irrationality inherent in the ecological and urban crises which led to a breakdown of order and threatened normal social patterns. These crises

> ". . . created widespread fear, resent-
> ment, and anger in the working and
> middle classes; but this anger, instead
> of venting itself against the corpora-
> tions, too often finds secondary tar-
> gets - the Blacks, liberals, radical
> students 'bureaucracy,' 'government
> interference.' The Left then misinter-
> prets the symptoms of popular resentment
> as incorrigible racism, devotion to the
> status quo, and proto-facism, and writes
> off the working class and new middle
> class as reactionary."[1]

What Lasch omits from his analysis is crucial. Of course, the Student Movement evolved into a secretarian force guided by a cultural critique which called for a massive evasion of the dominant social institutions. But what is more important is the theoretical directions outlined by those intellectuals that surrounded the New Left Idea. Their work was an attempt to explain the dynamics of political consciousness and its cultural configuration that condition the working class' response to the breakdown of social order and the failure of liberal solutions. Why does the working class respond to the collapse of order by 'finding secondary targets and falling prey to the disunifying cancer of racism'? What ideological and cultural prerequisites shape this response instead of a general outrage with the corporate

---

[1] Ibid., pg. 116.

state? Has it been [in Marcusean terms] some 'biological' transition of the instincts under late capitalism? Is that instinctual? Or is it a general pattern of constant socialization to the blind - or fearful - acceptance of social hierarchy and political power? These questions, and more, must be confronted in assessing the full thrust of the New Left - its movements and ideas - if such an analysis is to be considered a comprehensive effort.

Just when Lasch seems to be approaching some critical review of the New Left Idea, he falls back into the stereotyped categories of less incisive studies of the New Left. In another essay in The World of Nations entitled "After the New Left," Lasch writes:

> "A major theoretical problem for the New Left was precisely to work out a new conception of social reconstruction, in other words to formulate new ideas about revolution itself instead of being content with unanalyzed images from the past."[1]

But clearly the works of Mills, Marcuse, Baran and Sweezy, O'Connor and Gorz were an initial attempt at such a reconstruction. Suddenly Lasch shoves us back into the historically stale interpretation of the New Left as a movement without ideas. Rather it is the quality and quantity of those ideas which are at question.

Somehow much of Lasch's analysis of the New Left - as well as Clecak's - seems bound by a transitional character. Although both critics seem on the threshold of a fresh socio-political paradigm, their works reflect an indebtedness to the more traditional social democratic and neomarxist analyses. Indeed Lasch's closing paragraph in "After the New Left" indicates this.

---

[1] C. Lasch, "After the New Left," Ibid., pg. 126.

"But it is precisely tactical realism, a
respect for the commonplace, and renewed
attention to the way in which the crisis
of modern society is rooted in the
deteriorating conditions of everyday
life that the Left most urgently needs
to acquire."[1]

Lasch is calling for a more systematic study in
the relationship between society and culture
which

". . . is one of the most outstanding
weaknesses of classical Marxism. In
seeking to overcome it, we shall have to
confront not only the full complexity of
the historical record itself but a long
tradition of conservative criticism of
modern culture that has too often been
ignored by the Left."[2]

In doing so Lasch will necessarily have to review
the intellectual foundation of the American
Student Movement and he will have to attempt some
comprehensive presentation of the theoretical contours of the New Left Idea. Apparently Lasch's
present essays on narcisism mark a new beginning
for him.[3]

Clecak and Lasch represent the more lucid
theoretical thinking of those critical of the New
Left. In contrast, a range of literature simply
dismisses the New Left because of its political
style or lack of a coherent ideological perspec-

---

[1]Ibid., pg. 159

[2]Ibid., pg. 202.

[3]See Christopher Lasch, The Culture of Narcisism
(New York, 1979).

211

tive.[1] In general the critical literature simply has not taken up the main intellectual currents of the New Left Idea and challenged their theoretical consistency or empirical validity.

---

[1]Some examples are: Gil Green, op cit.; Irving Howe "New Styles in Leftism" from Dissent, Summer 1964 reprinted in Jacobs and Landau, op cit.; Jack Woddis, op cit.; Jack Barnes, et al., Towards An American Socialist Revolution (New York: Pathfinder, 1971); John P. Diggins, The American Left in the Twentieth Century (New York: Harcourt, 1973).

Chapter Eleven
The Contradictions of New Left Marxism

The New Left Idea identifies the political significance of the sociological, cultural and psychological underpinnings of contemporary capitalism. It establishes the relationship between the economic growth and stability of capitalism on the one hand, and on the other, the importance of the everyday life rituals, compulsions, and fantasies in the maintenance and reproduction of a social consciousness compatible with modern capitalism.

In attempting to unravel this relationship between what Mills termed the "public and private" dimensions of personal experience, the New Left Idea reverted to an unnecessary reliance on Freudian naturalism. The mainstay of this focus was the Marcusean influence - itself a product of Reich, Horkheimer, Schiller and several others. In the American context "cultural marxism" was rooted in a "freudian-marxism," and it was not until after the eclipse of the Student Movement that alternative directions for American cultural marxism began to emerge.

Marcuse attempted to avoid the reproduction Freud's naturalistic basis by constructing an historically distinct interpretaton of his theory of instincts. By replacing Freud's "reality principle" with his own "performance principle," Marcuse sought the construction of a politically and economically distinct social theory which identified the necessary psychological makeup and required cultural milieux that are unique for each stage of history. However, Marcuse's major works do not establish a class analysis within the general context of his cultural theory. He puts forth an explanation of the configuration of mass consciousness that does not specify the unique forms of reification distinct to each class. In general, class forms of alienation, exploitation and reification are absent from his social theory. His work focuses on the individual as the unit of

213

analysis and disregards class as a primary category.

In a more general sense Marcuse's perspective on this question seems to follow from his roots in the freudian-marxist circles of what is popularly known as the "Frankfurt School." As Tim Patterson has pointed out in a perceptive essay on this subject, the 'psycho-social Marsixts' present a theory of personality within a specific historical epoch, but they failed to address their original question which centered on the demise of working class consciousness.[1]

> "Starting from the observation that the forces of class conflict have been blunted in modern industrial capitalist societies, they proceed to the (usually unexpressed) position that classes are not very important, and this falls into a subtle reification of class consciousness, reducing it to a question of individual, internal processes, however generalized or common."[2]

Patterson's criticism of the "freudian-marxists" is somewhat exaggerated. Marcuse and his European colleagues focused on the masses of society and they were clearly not extending their analysis to those strata which commanded the politico-economic apparatus of modern society. However it is fair to argue, I believe, that the reliance of Marcuse, et al., on a general theory of personality and instincts led them away from a more specific analysis of the forms of cultural hegemony characteristic of various social categories - race, sex, intra-class rankings - within the general mass of society.

---

[1]See, Tim Patterson, "Notes on the Historical Application of Marxist Cultural Theory," Science and Society, Vol. 39, No. 3 Fall 1975, pgs. 257-291.

[2]Ibid., pg. 273.

A more important dimension of Marcuse's reliance on instinctual theory is his projection of the totalitarian character of the American political system. Marcuse asserted that the re-programming of the instinctual makeup of the individual created a redefinition of needs such that they are 'totally' compatible with the vested interests of the dominant institutional forces of advanced technological society. All opposition is eliminated as a viable force for change. This "one diemnsional society is reduced to a closed political universe."

Marcuse's concept of one dimensionality was a critical step in the development of a new praxis appropriate for late capitalism in the United States. He is guilty of several erroneous assumptions concerning political economy, he over-states the hegemony of the "ruling ideas," and his concept of one dimensionality incorrectly pre-cludes the existence of any type of unique working class consciousness. Yet even with each of these "false" premises Marcuse uncovers - or rather rediscovers - the political nature of culture and the importance of ideological hegemony to advanced capitalist society. Marcuse attempts to translate Marx's concept of ideological hegemony (The German Ideology) and identify its peculiar American character and contemporary consequences. However, Marcuse's analysis denied the working class its own subjectivity in the development of a world view and a compatible behavior pattern.

Marcuse's conclusion of the complete integra-tion of the working class into the system can be maintained without characterizing its domination as totalitarian. Henri Lefebvre, French sociolo-gist, has written at length on Marx's concept of praxis, and his work aids in the general assess-ment of the concept for the modern world, and offers a sociological context for an assessment of Marcuse. To Marx practice is separated from praxis because of its anti-theoretical and anti-intellectual character. Lefebvre writes:

"The criterion of practice, formulated in the second of the Theses on Feuerbach, will later be interpreted as a total rejection of theory in favor of practicality, as adherence to empiricism and the cult of efficiency, as a kind of pragmatism."[1]

Praxis, in contrast, reaffirms the philosophical, the intellectual by giving it a sensuous life. Praxis unites theory and practice, consequently it "rehabilitates" the sensuous by providing "the unity of the sensuous and the intellectual . . .".[2]

Within this context, Lefebvre argues that praxis involves the "dialectical relation between man and nature, consciousness and things. . .".[3] It is primarily "action." Every society involves a praxis because praxis is both content and the forms created by this content. In short, all societies are based on some set of ideas and present those ideas as actions, thereby creating their forms. Capitalist society creates the commodity form which is never separated from its content because labor is simultaneously a use and exchange value. "The form is fetishized. It appears as a thing endowed with boundless powers."[4] By relying on Lefebvre's analysis one can begin an evaluation of the potential of Marcuse's one dimensionality. Lefebvre asserts that this unity of content and form under capitalism, which results in its fetish, "generates real apperances that befog 'reality' (praxis) the more

---

Henri Lefebvre, The Sociology of Marx, (Vintage, New York, 1969) pg. 34.

[2] Ibid., pg. 38.

[3] Ibid., pg. 45.

[4] Ibid., pg. 47.

effectively because they are part of it."[1] One can interpret Lefebvre as asserting that the mystification of consciousness, the obliteration of two dimensional society, lies within the unique character of capitalism's social construction. This leads to the position that the unification of opposites under capitalism is profound, for here labor is both use and exchange value, the simultaneous source of production and consumption, the necessary element of the system and its integrating factor while concomitantly the disintegrating element, the potential Revolutionary Subject. Capitalism's praxis contains these antagonisms by offering them a coherence in its very foundation - the everyday reaffirmation of its own logic, the rationality of its irrationality.

Lefebvre has identified three levels of praxis. Repetitive praxis performs the same acts "within determined cycles."[2] Mimetic praxis imitates without knowing or creating. Creative praxis is revolutionary activity which "introduces concrete (dialectical) intelligibility into social relations."[3] Moreover, creative praxis brings "social forms into accord with their contents."[4] But in this sense, revolutionary praxis confronts the "conservative" praxis of capitalism.

Lefebvre's analysis expands the concept of praxis while attempting to preserve its Marxist orientation. Since all societies involve a praxis, capitalism's ideological strength is based on the repetitive and mimetic levels of praxis. Capitalism accomplishes the containment of its contradictions by the reproduction of its own logic and its daily reaffirmation; that is, monopoly capitalism requires a practice that is

---

[1] Ibid., pg. 47.

[2] Ibid., pg. 52.

[3] Ibid., pg. 53.

[4] Ibid., pg. 53.

itself rooted in the everyday life and the constant repetition of its sociological and political hierarchy. To Lefebvre capitalism's praxis is not simply economic production, but as Marx clearly outlined, it is also the production of a world view and its general ethical and spiritual values. Production is mimetic and repetitive. As Lefebvre writes in his Everyday Life in the Modern World, production implies reproduction.[1] It is not only biological reproduction but economic, technical and social. Social reproduction involves the interplay of a variety impulse generating a social impulse. In his words,

"... this impulse, this many-faceted phenomenon that affects objects and beings, which controls nature and adapts it to humanity, this praxis and poiesis does not take place in the higher spheres of a society (state, scholarship, 'culture') but in everyday life."[2]

It seems reasonable for one to conclude that existence is non authentic within the one dimensional society described by Marcuse. The libidinal totalitarianism of modern capitalism precludes authenticity since it denies "self." In the conquest of the "private," the one dimensional society is paradoxically characterized by social atomization. Within the universality of monopoly capitalism, people are separated sociologically and aesthetically while their needs and instincts are simultaneously homogenized. To Marcuse contradictions pertain within this society and only revolutionary praxis can restore real creativity, hence authenticity. As Martin Jay has written:

---

[1]Henri Lefebvre, Everyday Life in the Modern World (New York: Harper and Row, 1969).

[2]Ibid., pg. 31.

218

"To Marcuse, man can exist authentically only by performing radical deeds, only by engaging in self creating praxis."[1] The need for authenticity is at once created by the ideological machinations of the cultural apparatus and simultaneously frustrated by the failure of its realization through the commodity form. This is one aspect of Marcuse's "contradictions." "The result," in Bruce Brown's formulation, "is an explosive collision between the claims of human instinct and a civilization that continues to deny them."[2]

The kinds of unsatisfied needs in one dimensional society relate to the qualitative rather than the material realm of existence. According to Marcuse, the political economic apparatus will maintain an ever increasing surplus and hence continuous wealth and growth. It is with the notion of authenticity that modern capitalism falters. Authenticity is to be achieved within the parameters of the commodity form and the repressive social arrangements; however, this is a basic contradiction, for authenticity implies subjectivity, while the commodity form offers only objectivity and reification. Authenticity is beyond the capability of the system while the mimetic praxis of late capitalism is shrouded in a cloak of individualism and atomized consumerism that promises authentic experience as its reward. There is no authenticity without subjectivity. There is no subjectivity in Marcuse's libidinal totalitarianism, because subjectivity presupposes consciousness, and all consciousness in the one dimensional society is false. It is anti-life, anti-eros. "One dimensionality creates its own specific form of immediate negative experience,"

---

[1] Martin Jay, "How Utopian is Marcuse," in George Fisher, ed., The Revival of American Socialism (New York: Oxford University Press, 1971), pg. 246.

[2] Brown, op cit., pg. 25.

219

Jeremy Shapiro has written, " which is best articulated in such writiers as Kafka and Sartre:
absurdity, nausea, superfluity, meaninglessness,
schizophrenia, being lost in existence."[1]

Revolutionary praxis assumes subjectivity and
creativity. It is my contention that the New Left
and the American Student Movement developed a
practice which sought this subjectivity and creativity. They attempted the construction of a
practice - unfortunately they never developed a
legitimate revolutionary praxis - which would
produce fundamental social change. The New Left
Idea assumed that changes in consciousness and
everyday life must preceed political revolution.[2]
The New Left Idea designed a potential praxis
which would focus on the everyday life and the
structure of personality by demanding changes in
the individual's private realm as a necessary step
in the process of social transformation of the
"public" realm. On this topic, the intellectual
and political history of the New Left and the
Student Movement coincide. They sought "total"
changes in the individual as preconditions for
changes in society. Individual change

> "constitutes praxis not as immediate
> action upon society, but as part of the
> creation of the new subject."[3]

---

[1] Jeremy Shapiro, "One Dimensionality: The Universal Semiotic of Technological Experience," in Paul
Breines, op cit., p. 175.

[2] For an extended presentation see Karl Klare.
"The Critique of Everyday Life, the New Left and
the Unrecognizable Marxism" in Karl Klare and Dick
Howard, editors, The Unknown Dimension, European
Marxism Since Lenin (New York: Basic Books, Inc.,
1972).

[3] Shierry Weber, "Individuation as Praxis," in
Breines, op cit., pg. 58.

In this way, revolutionary praxis becomes the opposite of Freud's repressive dialectic involving the renunciation of the life instincts, but rather praxis became the individual's reaffirmation of his own subjectivity. However, New Left practice became the opposite of revolutionary practice by sliding back into either the Old Left puritanism (unswerving adulation of the working class, regardless of its political position) or the anarcho-cultural evasion of the dominant social praxis (e.g. the Weatherman).

If Lefebvre's concept of mimetic praxis may be applied to the American context, it suggests to me a more satisfactory description of contemporary class consciousness. For to argue that individual personality has been totally absorbed by the cultural apparatus is itself "false" because it forecloses the subjective element for all historical purposes; rather, modern consciousness may be described as the conscious mimic of the "ruling ideas" either for reasons of political pragmatism, cultural manipulation, or social indifference. But in each case the conscious choice is made - the decision to imitate those values dominant within the cultural milieux. "Mime" is qualitatively distinct from the condition of libidinal control. Marcuse denies the working class the subjective quality of conscious integration within the advanced technological system.

This distinction is critical because it illuminates the processes developing false consciousness and mimetic praxis. Marcuse asserted the "total" absorbtion of the personality by the political, cultural and ideological rationalization of advanced capitalism. At worst this precludes any logical break with this system and, at best, the chances of liberation are slim. According to Marcuse at some point the system would create insatiable needs within the capitalist system and consequently a political collision would occur between the needs generated by that system and its repressive forms of control. Contrary to Marcuse it is perfectly logical to assert that the cooptive and repressive powers of the system will simply redefine needs and create new "commodities" for their satisfaction. The individual is denied experience hence denied choice. Why should he suddenly develop such foreign behavior?

If, however, contemporary social consciousness is mimetic rather than one dimensional, it may be more readily reversed because it is essentially conditioned by the everyday submission to the political and economic domination of advanced capitalism. Alienation can only be ameliorated - however briefly - through the commodity form because the political and economic supremacy of the system preclude any alternatives, because the only significant "free choice" appears to lie in the area of consumption. The mimetic system rests not on libidinal domination but rather on the containment of the subjective forces, both intellectual and political. Within the mimetic system, personality is perverted by the daily compromises and submissions to hierarchial order, consequently the focus on the relationship between the political socio-economic forces and the individual personality remains critical for any thorough understanding of modern social consciousness. However, this is a qualitatively different condition from Marcuse's one dimensionality. In short, cultural hegemony simultaneously results from the political and economic domination of the objective forces as well as the subjective act of deference to authority.

By utilizing Lefebvre's concept of mimetic praxis as a starting point, one can construct an alternative "cultural" analysis to that of Marcuse. The mimetic system begins to falter when either its ideological rationality breaks down or its economic base suffers a significant disruption. Conservative social consciousness ebbs because the supremacy of the system is reduced to myth. To Marcuse when the one dimensional system proved incapable of satisfying its goals, it seems more likely that the conditioned libidos would seek a restoration of the existing structure of economic benefit rather than seek qualitatively unique social arrangements.

Contrary to Marcuse's one dimensionality, a political analysis built on the concept of mimetic praxis is more internally consistent with the realities of subjective and objective forces. By starting with Lefebvre's concept, but going well beyond his initial premises one can integrate much of the New Left Idea with an extended analysis of mimetic praxis. Mimetic consciousness rests on the subtle wearing down of the individual's sense of historical relevance. The everyday patterns of hierarchial domination forge the general perception of powerlessness. The individual perceives his world as totally determined by forces outside of his immediate world, hence the separation of the public issues and private troubles described by Mills. The individual's introjection of the political and economic domination, inherent in the modern situation, produces the possibility of a cultural environment characterized by the submission of individuals to commodities and their projected illusions and fantasies. It is not these commodities which are the source of domination but rather the continuing condition of labor as a commodity and the maintenance of this status by a growing political apparatus. Mimetic consciousness is a function of the concentration of bureaucratic and police power accompanied by its intellectual and cultural intermediaries. In the mimetic world, submission and introjection are supremely pragmatic for the working class individual, which results in a general sense of inferiority and everyday terror that only strengthens the submissive impulses.

Mimetic praxis then is an ideological analysis of the cultural domination of social consciousness. This is quite different from the "freudian-marxist" interpretation which is founded on an instinctual theory. The ideological analysis permits the retention of class as the critical unit of analysis and this approach projects the question of class consciousness in a non-deterministic political framework.

In addition to its cultural weaknesses the New Left Idea was similarly burdened by the undeveloped character of a good portion of its political economy. In many essays the New Left appeared to accept uncritically many of the assumptions of the post-scarcity or "post industrial" argument. Specifically, the New Left accepted the prosperity encountered by the United States and Europe in the post war period as the unalterable face of the future. In ironic manner, Daniel Bell's "end of ideology" economics seems to have subconsciously crept into the economic thinking of many who were bent on disproving the non-ideological character of "developed" society. The inherent tendency towards economic crisis, which plagues any capitalist order, was temporarily sidestepped by many New Leftists. Baran and Sweezy, of course, were not in this number, but many of their interpreters were, most particularly those insistent on the disaccumulation theory of advanced capitalism.

One of the effects of the New Left's embryonic political economy led to the failure to resolve the question of agency for social change. The category of class - although surveyed and debated - was never appropriately defined or redefined. The changes in the character of work - non manual, paraprofessional and professional - were mistakenly identified as the rise of a "new" class. Educated labor was perceived in some New Left quarters as a new class instead of a shift within a class. Were the relationships between the worker and work substantively altered? Was the worker structurally redefined in relation to the workplace? To the control of work? The revised ratio between manual and non manual work, primary and infrastructural employment, were simply described in sociological terms by the New Left.

The failure to resolve the question of class resulted in the New Left's inability to develop a comprehensive understanding of racism. Because the New Left Idea did not develop an economic and historical framework for interpreting the contemporary significance of racism and its relationship to a class analysis, it segregated the racial phenomenon from its general political analysis. Racism remained an all purpose additive to various critiques of the American system. It was treated in either a moralistic manner (the ERAP experience; the "white skin priviledge" of the Weathermen) or it was absent from the root of the analysis (e.g. One Dimensional Man).[1] The missing theoretical understanding of the economic and historical significance of American racism blunted the political economy of the New Left and precluded a comprehensive cultural critique.

The crucial breakthrough which the New Left represents for the marxist and neo-marxist heritage is the identification of the cultural foundation of advanced capitalism as significant as the economic base in the formation of a national consensus under modern capitalism. The New Left Idea outlines the relationship between the economic framework of the system and its critical reliance on the sociological, political, and psychological dimensions. Thus, the New Left Idea was an attempt to specify the "totalistic" domination and coordination of human experience necessary for the maintenance and growth of capitalism. "Societies must be understood simultaneously as functional totalities," writes Bruce Brown

". . . characterized by a particular social and technical division of labor and mode of exploitation and as affective totalities, whose driving elements

---

[1]Some exceptions are notable, namely: chapter nine, "Monopoly Capitalism and Race Relations" in Baran and Sweezy, Monopoly Capital, op cit.; Harold M. Baran, "The Demand for Black Labor: Historical Notes on the Political Economy of Racism," Radical America (Vol. 5, No. 2 March-April 1971); a lengthy analysis appearing in the radical newsweekly, The Guardian, later presented in book form by Robert Allen, Black Awakening in Capitalist America (New York: Doubleday, 1969).

are feelings and desires, fears and
anxieties, fantasies and dreams, etc."[1]

Brown argues that conventional Marxist analysis presents a limited explanation of what is a
complex web of social, political, pshcyological
and economic relationships. To Brown this
approach explains the cultural dimension (and the
full spectrum of the superstructure) as a consequence of the forms of domination set out in the
base structure of the social order. Freudian-
marxism is founded in the identification of the

". . . natural basis of the human
species as essentially determined by the
rechanneling of surplus impulses and by
extended childhood dependence . . .".[2]

The stability of advanced capitalism is
founded on the repressive character of psychological and social relationships. Everyday life for
the individual is a series of evasions, compulsions and adaptations. The individual's 'survival' demands his acceptance of the dominance of
the social order over his public and private
decisions, and his fear of not surviving - at
least in terms of social acceptance and conformity - instills within the individual feelings
of terror. Daily life is characterized by the
individual's attempt to "make his peace with the
system" by resorting to a readily available array
of mechanisms which offer him the security of
escape and fantasy, a task made easy in a mass
consumption culture.

The New Left Idea projected the failure of
revolutionary consciousness as a consequence of
the obliteration of the 'private' by the 'public'
sphere whereby "spontaneous" behavior is reduced
to system supportive evasion and fantasy. The
resurgence of revolutionary praxis flows from the

---

[1]Bruce Brown, op cit., pg. 71.

[2]Ibid., pgs. 84-85.

226

growing awareness of the central contradiction of late capitalism: that future repression and self-denial is unnecessary within the context of a society which possesses the technological capability to transcend scarcity. The realization of this contradiction and its resolution are dependent on the subjective elements of political organization and revolutionary praxis.

The New Left Idea was burdened by an unhealthy reliance on the naturalistic framework of the Freudian theory of instincts, the undeveloped character of its political economy and the undefined aspects of its evaluation of the question of class and social agency. However, the idea represents a major juncture in the evolution of a reinvigorated marxism and the construction of a new theory of praxis. It a is mistake to relegate the Idea and the Movement, as Clecak and Lasch do, to intellectual and social obscurity, as a mere spontaneous radical interruption in the continuity of the status quo.

American capitalism has been able to develop a system-supportive social consciousness because its sociological context maintains the distinctions between public and private life, but in a new way. The interpretation of experience is constantly influenced by the vested interests of the cultural apparatus such that all areas formerly regarded as private are now easily invaded by these public intrusions and attempts at manipulation. The patterns of leisure and everyday life are significant arenas for social control and repression and not merely adjunct activities within the context of the repressive world of work relations. If the New Left Idea offered any new directions for the understanding of contemporary social reality, it was clearly the identification of the importance of the interrelationship between the private and the public domains in the maintenance and growth of modern capitalism. Its strength grows from its ability to rationalize an irrational system with limited recourse to violence and coercion.

Driven by the need to expand markets in the face of economic surplus, the capitalist system, with the orchestration and underwriting of the State apparatus, pursues the centralization of production and distribution. It comes to rely on the expansion of markets through the coordination and prodding of the cultural apparatus. This cultural milieu in conjunction with the hierarchial organization of work, leisure, and the bulk of the socialization apparatus, defines and refines the mass consumer markets while disciplining and multi-racial work force which lies at the core of the system. The corporate colonization of work and leisure serves to contain and minimize the subjective elment. The hierarchial bureaucratic organization of techno-corporate capitalism expands its control over the domains of work, consumption and leisure. The private domain contracts in the face of the expanded public arena. Everyday life is an integral apsect of consumption patterns and consequently a crucial target for the corporate state as it seeks to maximize profit, minimize cost and avoid the hazards of rapid change.

Chapter Twelve
Towards a New Theory of Praxis

The New Left Idea represented a major break-through in the development of a new theory of praxis for the American context because it expanded the forms of contemporary political economy beyond the institutional limits of the Old Left heritage. It attempted to explain the question of consciousness development instead of simply dismissing non-revolutionary proletarian consciousness as "false." It allowed us to look at the total environment of the working class in order to uncover the forms of social control and ideological development. The sociological institutions of capitalism can be perceived as politically necessary for the present constitution of the system.

The New Left never developed a theory of praxis. The New Left Idea was composed of a collection of negations concerning modern capitalist praxis and a set of ideas about future praxis. The value of the New Left Idea is heuristic for it offers the possibility of the development of a new theory of praxis. This realization is, in part, dependent on the extension of the New Left Idea through the integration of its more salient features with the writings of a number of theorists concerned with the dialectics of modern capitalism.

The New Left Idea rediscovered the "totalistic" nature of marxism, for it was Marx who wrote:

"Man, much as he may therefore be a particular individual . . . is just as much the totality - the ideal totality - the subjective existence of thought and experienced society present for itself."[1]

---

[1] K. Marx, 1844 Manuscripts, quoted in Bertell Ollman, op cit., pg. 22.

229

The New Left Idea reaffirmed Marx's social theory
as one of internal relations instead of more
narrowly$_1$ constructed critique of political
economy.^{1} It reaffirmed the subjective dimensions
of Marx's writings and in this regard the integration of the work of George Lukacs, Henri Lefebvre,
Antonio Gramaci, and several others extends the
New Left Idea beyond its present role of isolated
critique. These writers were, and are, concerned
with broadening the marxist theoretical focus to
include a significant emphasis on the question sof
cultural hegemony, reification and the revival of
the subjective forces as necessary elements in the
construction of a new theory of praxis which seeks
the transformation of present social reality. It
is this initial integration which simultaneously
adds to the historical importance of the New Left
Idea and traces the outline for a new theory.

Reification as Social Control

        The New Left Idea, as noted, was bur-
dened by its instinctual assumptions about the
nature of man. However resourceful the attempt to
temporalize a theory of instincts - as Marcuse
sets out to achieve with his performance principle - it is basically founded on a set concept
of the nature of man and consequently it can be
reduced to an a-historical deterministic theoretical construct. Regardless of its modified form,
instinctual theory decreases the importance of the
subjective forces within the historical process.
Praxis is thus diminished as a force for social
change.

---

^{1}For a comprehensive treatment of this subject
see, B. Ollman, op cit., Ollman's basic thesis
concerns the establishement of Marx's theory of
internal relations where every major variable of
superstructure and base is internal to each other
and consequently each of these variables is significant but none is deterministic.

Instinctual theories of history are attempted answers to the classical philosophical inquiry, "What is man?" It assembles a politico-biological response to what is a dialectical historical question. As Antonio Gramsci wrote:

"When we consider it, we find that by putting the question 'What is man?' we really mean, "What can man become?', that is, whether or not man can control his own destiny, can 'make himself,' can create a life for himself."[1]

The human experience is defined by a set of interactions with other men, nature, and the individual himself. Man is a reflection of the totality of these interactions, and he changes to the extent that he changes his relationship with all these forces.

"If individuality is the whole mass of these relationships, the acquiring of a personality means the acquiring of consciousness of these relationships, and changing the personality means changing the whole mass of these rela- tionships."[2]

In addition, the historical heritage of all these relationships influences any definition of present man. From this perspective philosophy always retains a political dimension. The interactions of diverse individuals, groups, institutions, and histories are bound by a dialectical unity where man is always in the stage of "becoming." In- stinctual theories of man limit the dialectical nature of human relationships.

---

[1]Antonio Gramsci, The Modern Prince and Other Writings, (New York; International Publishers, 1970), pg. 76.

[2]Ibid., pg. 77.

Within the Marxist framework, the changes which occur in the economic foundation that 'lead sooner or later' to changes in the totality of the superstructure are prompted and realized because of a revolutionary praxis. "History is characterized by the growth and development of needs," as Lefebvre states.[1] But the concept of praxis presupposes the conscious exertion of human will within the historical process in order to realize a new social order. This is quite different from asserting that pure biological determinants and manipulations define and identify human activity within and between each discrete epoch of mankind. According to Marx's theory of praxis, social changes occur when objective possibilities can be achieved during specific historical moments while society becomes conscious of these possibilities and the irrational nature of their place within the contemporary configuration of the social order. Conscious social activity alters the present form of social activity in a revolutionary way.

In his discussion of the stages of consciousness development by the working class, Lukacs asserted that the first step involves a subjective realization that:

". . . In every aspect of daily life in which the individual worker imagines himself to be the subject of his own life he finds this to be an illusion that is destroyed by the immediacy of his existence."[2]

Although the totality of his existence is dominated by the reification of all his relationships, the proletarian's fate need not be explained as

---

[1]Henri Lefebvre, The Sociology of Marx, op cit., pg. 42.

[2]George Lukacs, History and Class Consciousness (Cambridge: MIT Press, 1971), pg. 165.

the 'biological' reprogramming of his instincts but simply his realization that he has been reduced to a mere object in the production and consumption processes.

"The quantification of objects, their subordination to abstract mental categories makes its appearance in the life of the worker immediately as a process of abstraction of which he is the victim. . .".[1]

He is separated from his labor power, forced to sell it as a commodity:

"And by selling this, his only commodity, he integrates it (and himself: for his commodity is inseperable from his physical existence) into a specialized process that has been rationalized and mechanized, a process that he discoveres already existing, complete and able to function without him and in which he is no more than a cipher reduced to an abstract quantity, a mechanized and rationalised tool."[2]

In short, the worker internalizes the commodity form through the process of inversion.[3]

Reification can be overcome, according to Lukacs, ". . . only by constant and constantly renewed efforts to disrupt the reified structure of existence by relating to the concretely manifested contradictions of the total development, by becoming conscious of the immanent meanings of these contradictions for the total develop-

---

[1] Ibid., pg. 165.
[2] Ibid., pg. 166.
[3] Marx, Grundrisse, op cit., pgs. 831-832.

233

ment."[1]   Lukacs   restated   Marx's   concept   of
"totality" in the theory of alienation, first
outlined in the <u>Manuscripts of 1844</u>. The New Left
Idea popularly introduced this construct of
"totality" within the American context.

It   is   this   "total"   focus   on   the
processes of exploitation and alienation that
points to the importance of 'Everyday' existence.
The New Left Idea identified as important the
non-work institutions of the social superstructure
which perform these mediations and help achieve
and solidify the process of inversion.

> "The   main   institutions   within   and
> against which the individual confronts
> society prior to entering the work-
> world,"

according to Stanley Aronowitz

> "are family, schools, religion and more
> recenlty, mass culture. These institu-
> tions mediate between the social rela-
> tions   of   production   and   individual
> consciousness by communicating to the
> individual   his   place   in   the   social
> division of labor while providing con-
> trary symbols that hold out the pos-
> sibility of transcending the fate of
> previous generations."[2]

These institutions condition the expectations,
attitudes and personal identities in such a manner
as to attempt to influence social consciousness
and social behavior in conformity with the vested
interests of a system of class domination and
hierarchy. In order to comprehend the function-

---

[1]Lukacs, <u>op</u> <u>cit</u>., pg. 197.

[2]Stanley Aronowitz, <u>False Promises, The Shaping of</u>
<u>American Working Class Consciousness</u> (New York:
McGraw-Hill, 1973), pg. 10.

ing of the system, the status of class consciousness and the probabilities of social change, the institutions of the superstructure, which are mostly repsonsible for the mediations between the worker and the system, must be accounted for in a comprehensive analytic social theory. The major importance of the New Left Idea is that it initiated this intellectual focus for the American marxist and neo-marxist heritage.

Mediations and Cultural Hegemony

The critical mediations of the superstructure and the configuration of relationships which constitute social relations in the base foundation of late capitalism, together, form what Marx and then Lenin and Gramsci termed the intellectual[1] and cultural hegemony of the capitalist system. In the German Ideology Marx and Engels outline the importance of the intellectual domination of any society by the 'ruling ideas' of that society's ruling class. In the Introduction to the Critique of Political Economy, Marx further identifies the reciprocal relationship between the relations in the base structure of society and the cultural milieu which frames its social formations. The specific base configuration will determine the variety of social possibilities that make up the "totality" of everyday life experiences.

In contemporary capitalism, the institutions of mediation form a moral and, broadly defined, intellectual bloc which conditions and modifies the behavior of individuals of all classes. The continuous experience with all these institutions is the constant theme of individual

---

[1]See Antonio Gramsci, Selections from the Prison Notebooks (New York: International Publishers, 1971). and Antonio Gramsci, The Modern Prince and Other Writings (New York: International Publishers, 1970).

deference to social hierarchy and political domination. Their universal message is that the working class individual is powerless to alter significantly the rules of this system and that liberation can be attained only by individual action through socially acceptable experience. Social action which challenges the fundamental underpinnings of the social structure is threatening to its stability. Such behavior and ideas must be treated either by a punitive reponse - repression - or they must be coopted by the system such that their value as oppositional forces are diluted (because their presentation legitimizes the "rules of the game" and thus the system itself). In a Marcusian sense, the basic operating principle of the capitalist cultural - and hence moral/ethical - framework is that all activity is possible as long as it can be packaged to the specifications of the dominant social hierarchy. This cultural hegemony pecludes the legitimacy of antagonistic forces as oppositionist activites. The message of this cultural environment is clearly that working class individuals and groups are powerless fundamentally to alter the configuration of class forces - all other activity is acceptable because by this rule all other activity can be packaged within the commodity form. Social consciousness precludes radical change because it falls outside the rationale of the system. Much like Heller's "Catch-22" logic, the rational solution to late capitalism means radical change, but "radical" activity and thinking are by definition irrational, hence under the cultural hegemony of capitalism, all attempts to change fundamentally an irrational system are themselves irrational. Or so goes the logic of its superstructure.

The reality of social hierarchy and its consequent trait of societal inferiority serve to preempt the perception of subjectivity from the significant political arenas of everyday life. The working class is painfully aware of its reduced ability to participate in the meaningful decisions which condition its social environment. It internalizes its powerlessness and it comes to see iteslf as mere objects in the major dimensions

236

of social history. Whether he confronts power in the arenas of general bureaucracy, work, school, government, and even popular culture, the individual understands his inferior social standing and political impotency.

There is really only one arena in which the individual is "free" to particpate in the modern world of capitalism and this occurs in the world of consumption. The choices over what to consume and in what quantities appear as the only subjective decisions available to the individual. Even within this context the reality of corporate domination is felt; however, the immediate selection of the commodity occurs within the boundaries of his immediate environment with the corporate apperances held to a minimum.

Within the world of consumption the individual adapts to the parameters of a hierarchically structured system of social domination by releasing his repressed subjectivity through a series of compulsive acts. The stocked aisles of the supermarket allow the individual to engage in a form of socially condoned participation where this sudden "freedom" releases a storehouse of desires and unfilled fantasies. Lefebvre has described this process as one of "fictitious" decision making.

"Such conflicts and problems of everyday life involve 'fictitious' solutions, superimposed on the 'real' solutions when these are, or seem to be, 'impossible.' Thus problems and the search for solutions overstep the frontier of make-believe; 'projections' unobtrusively fill the gap between experience and make-believe and people project their desires on to one group of objects or another, one form of activity or another; the home, the flat, furnishing, cooking, going away on holiday, 'nature,' etc. Such projections invest the

237

object with a double existence, real and imaginary."[1]

The world of consumption is not a compilation of mindless actions resulting from reprogrammed instincts but rather it represents a more complicated set of actions which stem from the unsatisfied needs of creativity and participation that can only be resolved under late capitalism through a subsystem of fictional decision making. The pent up compulsions stemming from political, social and psychological inferiority are thereby released in this form of social adaptation and conformity.[2]

The false nature of this participation is readily perceived by the individual, who painfully realizes that he is consuming not things but images fabricated by a self-interested cultural apparatus. Emptiness and frustration follow. As Lefebvre writes:

---

[1] Henri Lefebvre, Everyday Life in the Modern World, op cit., pg. 88.

[2] Richard Sennett and Jonathan Cobb discuss this topic in their recent study entitled The Hidden Injuries of Class (New York: Vintage, 1973). "The result of this [the psychological injuries of class], we believe, is that the activities which keep people moving in a class society, which make them seek more money, more possessions, higher-status jobs, do not originate in a materialistic desire, or even sensuous appreciation, of things, but out of an attempt to restore a psychological deprivation that the class structure has effected in their lives. In other words, the psychological motivation instilled by a class society is to heal a doubt about the self rather than create more power over things and other persons in the outer world . . .". (Pg. 171)

"How then can frustration and disappointment be avoided if people have nothing more substantial than signs to get their teeth into?[1]

Social Contradictions and Advanced Capitalism

And here lie the origins of a change in consciousness. It is within the disillusioning realm of consumption and false participation that the contradictions of late capitalism initially surface. It is at this stage that the hegemony of culture - its class interests and purposes - begin to emerge. The individual begins to become aware that it is he who is being consumed. However, the realization of the ficticious nature of consumption - and most decisions involved in everyday life - is not a sufficient condition to spark the urge for political revolt. The necessary agent is the realization of an attainable alternative society which will allow genuine participation and creativity.[2] This condition represents the subjective element of political organization which is nothing more than the development of a revolutionary praxis. Revolutionary change under late capitalism involves not only the awareness of

---

[1] Ibid., pg. 91.

[2] Andre Gorz in his Socialism and Revolution (New York: Anchor Books, 1973) speaks to this point in his extended essay on reform and revolution. "The demand for change, in other words, does not arise out of the impossibility of tolerating the existing state of affairs, but out of the possibility of no longer having to tolerate it. It is the demonstration of this possibility (whether immediate or not, and whether capable or not of being expressed in action), in every field of social and individual life, which is one of the basic elements in the ideological work of revolutionary movement." pgs. 167-168.

social contradictions but it also entails an analytic theory of the political and economic foundations of society and its processes, plus the practical outline of a political strategy and its appropriate tactics and activities. This is simply stated as the unity of theory and practice.

The revolutionary project is the creation of the intellectual possibilities and political probabilities that will challenge the praxis of social relations which maintain late capitalism and then substitute an alternative world view that calls for the realization of real participation (subjectivity) and creativity. A revolutionary culture with a new ethical and moral bloc must replace the cultural hegemony of the praxis on the capitalist order. The New Left Idea represents the initial stage in the development of a new theory of praxis for the American context because, at the very least, it identifies the reality of capitalist cultural hegemony as a necessary foundation for the rationalization and mediation of the capitalist order.

Revolutionary praxis under late capitalism must be anchored in the recognition of capitalist cultural hegemony and its forms of social control within everyday life. Any revolutionary theory of praxis must outline a political strategy for the programmatic assault on this problem of hegemony. The American New Left Student Movement ultimately developed a political style that led to a political assault on the dominant capitalist culture; however, the political counter culture of the sixties called for the evasion of the dominant culture and the erection of alternative communities and institutions which attempted to avoid the hegemony of the elite class. This strategy led the Movement away from any direct challenge to the legitimacy, ethics and morality of the capitalist culture. Any revolutionary movement must, as Bruce Brown points out:

> ". . . actualize itself through a new praxis aimed not at the 'evasion' of

everyday life, but at its 'transformation.'"[1]

A revolutionary praxis must be based on the construction of an analysis of the irrational character and omnipotent forms of isolation and disillusionment which are present in everyday life in our society. It must fashion a new world view that identifies the human possibilities for real participation and creativity within a defined rational alternative to the present social order. In the fashion of Antonio Gramsci's "Modern Prince" (the marxist political party) any revolutionary praxis for late capitalist society must erect political institutions and design political movements which:

". . . must and cannot but be the preacher and organizer of intellectual and moral reform, which means creating the basis for a later development of the national popular collective will towards the realization of a higher and total form of modern civilization."[2]

Conclusion

The New Left Idea in the American context represented a major intellectual development for the American radical heritage because it identifies the necessity politico-cultural analysis for any sophisticated understanding of contemporary capitalism. It identified the economic and political dynamics inherent in the system which account for the prime importance of the mediations and legitimizations performed by the institutions of the superstructure. The cultural

---

[1]Bruce Brown, op cit., pg. 182.

[2]Antonio Gramsci, The Modern Prince and Other Writings, op cit. (New York: International Publishers, 1970), pg. 139.

apparatus in our corporate state socializes the costs of social control, political legitimacy and economic investment. The New Left Idea outlined the relationship between the institutions in the modern capitalist era, and in doing so, it indicated the necessity for a new political praxis and identified its initial form.

BIBLIOGRAPHY

Adelson, Alan. SDS: A Profile, (New York: Scribner, 1972)

Allen, Robert. Black Awakening in Capitalist America, (New York: Doubleday, 1969)

Aronowitz, Stanley. False Promises, (New York: McGraw-Hill, 1973)

Avineri, Shlomo. The Social and Political Thought of Karl Marx, (London: Cambridge University Press, 1968)

Baran, Paul and Sweezy, Paul. Monopoly Capital, (New York: Monthly Review Press, 1966)

Bell, Daniel. The End of Ideology, (New York: Free Press, 1960)

Benello, C. George and Roussopoulos, Dimitrios, eds. The Case for Participatory Democracy, (New York: Gorssman Pub., 1971)

Bookchin, Murray. Post Scarcity Anarchism, (Berkeley: Ramparts Press, 1971)

Breines, Paul, ed. Critical Interruptions: New Left Perspectives on Herbert Marcuse, (New York: Herder & Herder, 1970)

Brown, Bruce. Marx, Freud and the Critique of Everyday Life, (New York: Monthly Review, 1973)

Calvert, Greg and Nieman, Carol. A Dirupted History, (New York: Random House, 1971).

Cammett, John. Antonio Gramsci and the Origins of Italian Communism, (Stanford: Stanford University Press, 1967)

Cleaver, Harry. Reading CAPITAL Politically, (Austin: University of Texas Press, 1979)

Clecak, Peter. Radical Paradoxes, (New York:
    Harper & Row, 1973)

Cohen, Mitchell and Hale, Dennis, eds. The New
    Student Left, (Boston: Beacon Press, 1967)

Diggins, John P. The American Left in the
    Twentieth Century, (New York: Harcourt,
    1973)

Ferbert, Michael and Lynd, Staughton. The Resis-
    tance, (Boston: Beacon Press, 1971)

Fisher, George, ed. The Revival of American
    Socialism, (New York: Oxford Press, 1971)

Freud, Sigmund. Civilization and Its Discontents,
    (New York: W. W. Norton, 1962)

Freud, Sigmund. Totem and Taboo, (New York: Vin-
    tage Books, 1946)

Ginsburg, Allen. Howl and Other Poems, (San Fran-
    cisco: City Lights Books, 1956)

Godelier, Maurice. Rationality and Irrationality
    in Economics, (New York: Monthly Review
    Press, 1973)

Goodman, Mitchell, ed. The Movement Toward a New
    America, (Philadelphia: Pilgrim Press, 1970)

Goodman, Paul. Growing Up Absurd, (New York:
    Vintage, 1960)

Gorz, Andre. Socialism and Revolution, (New York:
    Anchor Books, 1973)

Gorz, Andre. Strategy for Labor, (Boston: Beacon
    Press, 1967)

Gramsci, Antonio. The Modern Prince and Other
    Writings, (New York: International Publish-
    ers, 1970)

Green, Gil. The New Radicalism, (New York: Inter-
    national Publishers, 1971)

Harrington, Michael. Fragments of the Century, (New York: Saturday Review Press, 1973)

Harrington, Michael. The Twilight of Capitalism, (New York: Touchstone Books, 1978)

Higham, John. Writing American History, (Bloomington: Indiana University Press, 1970)

Hoffman, John. Marxism and the Theory of Praxis, (New York: International Publishers, 1975)

Horkhiemer, Max and Adorno, Theodor. The Dialectic of the Enlightenment, (New York: Continuum, 1972)

Horowitz, Irving Louis, ed. C. Wright Mills. Power, Politics and People, (London: Oxford University Press, 1963).

Howard, Dick and Klare, Michael, eds. The Unknown Dimension: European Marxism Since Lenin, (New York: Basic Books, 1972).

Jacobs, Harold, ed. Weatherman, (U.S.A.: Ramparts Press, 1970)

Jacobs, Paul and Landau, Saul, ed. The New Radicals, (New York: Vintage, 1966)

Jay, Martin. The Dialectical Imagination, (New York: Little & Brown, 1973)

Krim, Seymour. The Beats, (New York: Fawcett Pub., 1960)

Lasch, Christopher. The Agony of the American Left, (New York: Vintage Press, 1969)

Lasch, Christopher. The World of Nations, (New York: Vintage Press, 1974)

Lasch, Christopher. The Culture of Narcissism, (New York: Norton, 1979)

Lefebvre, Henry. Everyday Life in the Modern
    World, (New York: Harper & Row, 1969)

Lefebvre, Henry. The Sociology of Marx, (New
    York: Vintage, 1969)

Lenin, V. I. "Left Wing" Communism, An Infantile
    Disorder, (New York: International Pub.,
    1940)

Lenin, V. I. What Is to be Done, (New York:
    International Pub., 1969), second printing.

Lerner, Michael. The New Socialist Revolution,
    (New York: Dell Pub., 1973)

Lipset, Seymour and Wolin, Sheldon, eds. The
    Berkeley Student Revolt, (New York: Anchor
    Books, 1965)

Long, Priscilla, ed. The New Left, (Boston:
    Porter Sargent, 1969)

Lukacs, Georg. History and Class Consciousness,
    (Cambridge: MIT Press, 1971)

Mallet, Serge. Essays on the New Working Class,
    edited by Dick Howard and Dean Savage (St.
    Louis: Telos Press, 1975).

Mallet, Serge. La nouvelle classe ouvriere (Paris
    Editions due Seuil, 4th edition, 1969)

Mandel, Ernest. An Introduction to Marxist
    Economic Theory, (New York: Pathfinder
    Press, 1970)

Mandel, Ernest. Marxist Economic Theory, 2 vols.
    (New York: Monthly Review Pres, 1968)

Marcuse, Herbert. An Essay on Liberation,
    (Boston: Beacon Press, 1969)

Marcuse, Herbert. Counterrevolution and Revolt,
    (Boston: Beacon Press, 1972)

Marcuse, Herbert. Eros and Civilization, (Boston: Beacon Press, 1956)

Marcuse, Herbert. One Dimensional Man, (Boston: Beacon Press, 1964)

Marx, Karl. A Contribution to the Critique of Political Economy, (New York: International Pub., 1972)

Marx, Karl. Capital, Vol. I-II-III, (New York: International Pub., 1967).

Marx, Karl. Critique of the Gotha Programme, (New York: International Pub., 1970)

Marx, Karl. The Economic and Philosophic Manuscripts of 1844, Dirk J. Stanik (ed.), (New York: International Pub., 1964)

Marx, Karl. The Eighteenth Brumaire of Louis Bonaparte, (New York: International Pub., 1963).

Marx, Karl and Engels, Frederick. The German Ideology, (New York: International Pub., 1970)

Marx, Karl. The Grundrisse, M. Nicolaus, trans., (New York: Vintage Press, 1973).

Mattick, Paul. Critique of Marcuse: One Dimensional Man in Class Society, (New York: Herder & Herder, 1972)

Melman, Seymour. Pentagon Capitalism, (New York: McGraw-Hill, 1970)

Miles, Michael. The Radical Probe, The Logic of the Student Rebellion, (New York: Atheneum, 1973)

Mills, C. Wright. Power, Politics and People, ed. I. L. Horowitz, (London: Oxford University Press, 1963)

Mills, C. Wright. The Marxists, (New York: Dell Publishers, 1962)

Mills, C. Wright. The Power Elite, (New York: Oxford Press, 1959)

Mills, C. Wright. The Sociological Imagination, (New York: Oxford Press, 1959)

O'Connor, James. The Fiscal Crisis of the State, (New York: St. Martin's Press, 1973)

Ogelsby, Carl., ed. The New Left Reader, (New York: Grove Press, 1969)

Ollman, Bertell. Alienation: Marx's Concept of Man in Capitalist Society, (New York: Cambridge Press, 1971)

Potter, Paul. A Name for Ourselves, (New York: Little-Brown, 1971)

Richmond, Al. A Long View from the Left, (New York: Houghton-Mifflin, 1972)

Sale, Kirpatrick. SDS, (New York: Random House, 1973)

Sennett, Richard and Cobb, Jonathan. The Hidden Injuries of Class, (New York: Vintage Press, 1973).

Sherman, Howard. Radical Political Economy, (New York: BAsic Books, 1972)

Sigal, Clancey. Going Away, (New York: Dell Publishing Co., 1961)

Stolz, Mathew. The Politics of the New Left, (Beverly Hills: Glencoe Press, 1971)

Struik, Dirk, ed. Karl Marx. The Economic and Philosophic Manuscripts of 1844, (New York: International Publishers, 1964)

Swados, Harvey. Standing Fast, (New York:
    Doubleday, 1970)

Teodori, Massimo. The New Left: A Documentary
    Hitory, (New York: Bobbs Merrill, 1968)

Touraine, Alain. Post Industrial Society, (New
    York: Random House, 1971)

Unger, Irwin. The Movement: A History of the
    American New Left 1959-1972, (New York: Dodd
    & Mean, 1974)

Wallerstein, Immanual and Starr, Paul, ed. The
    University Crisis Reader, Vols. I & II, (New
    York: Random House, 1971).

Williams, William A. The Tragedy of American
    Diplomacy, (New York: Dell Pub., 1959)

Weinstein, James. Ambiguous Legacy: The Left in
    America, 1912-1925, (New York: Vintage
    Press, 1967).

Weinstein, James and Eakins, David, eds. For a
    New America, (New York: Vintage Books, 1970)

Woodis, Jack. New Theories of Revolution, (New
    York: International Publishers, 1972)

Zeitlin, Irving. Capitalism and Imperialism,
    (Chicago: Markham 1972).

Zeitlin, Irving. Marxism: A Re-Examination,
    (New York: Van Nostrand, 1967)

ARTICLES:

Aronson, Ronald. "Socialism: The Sustaining
    Menace," Studies on the Left, Vol. 6, No. 3,
    May-June 1966.

Aronson, Ronald. "The Movement and Its Critics,"
    Studies on the Left, Vol. 6, No. 1, January-
    February 1966.

Baxandall, Lee. "Issues and Constituency of the New Left," Liberation, April 1966.

Birnbaum, Norman and Lasch, Christopher. "America Today: An Exchange," Partisan Review, Vol. XLII, No. 3, 1975.

Boyte, Harry and Ackerman, Frank. "Revolution and Democracy," Socialist Revolution, Vol. 3, No. 4, July 1973.

Buhle, Paul. "The Eclipse of the New Left: Some Notes," Radical America, Vol. 6, No. 4, July 1972.

Fruchter, Norman and Kramer, Robert. "An Approach to Community Organizing," Studies on the Left, Vol. 6, No. 2, March-April, 1966.

Daniel Fusfeld. "The Rise of the Corporate State," Journal of Economic Issues, Vol. 1, No. 1, March 1972.

Genovese, Eugene. "Genovese Looks at the American Left - New and Old," The Guardian, February 1966.

Gintis, Herbert. "The New Working Class and Rev-olutionary Youth," Socialist Revolution, Vol. 1, No. 3, May, 1970.

Hunter, Allen and O'Brien, James. "Reading About the New Left," Radical America, Vol. 6, No. 4, July 1972.

Interim National Organizing Committee, New American Movement. "The New American Move-ment: A Way to Overcome the Mistakes of the Past," Socialist Revolution, Vol. 2, No. 1, January 1971.

Johnson, Dale L. "On the Ideology of the Campus Revolution," Studies On the Left, Vol. II, No. 1, 1961.

Judis, John. "From the New Left to a New
Socialist Party," Socialist Revolution, Vol.
3, No. 6, November 1973.

Judis, John. "The Personal and the Political,"
Socialist Revolution, #7 (Vol. 2, No. 1),
January-February, 1971.

Langer, Elinor. "Notes for Next Time: A Memoir
of the 1960's," Working Papers for a New
Society, Vol. 1, No. 3, Fall 1973.

Lichtheim, George. "From Marx to Hegel: Reflec-
tions on Georg Lukacs, T. W. Adorno, and
Herbert Marcuse," Triquarterly, No. 12,
Spring 1968.

Lichtman, Richard. "Marx's Theory of Ideology,"
Socialist Revolution, Vol. 5, No. 1, April
1975.

O'Brien, James. "Beyond Reminiscence: The New
Left in History," Radical America, Vol. 1,
No. 4, July 1972.

O'Connor, James. "Inflation, Fiscal Crisis and
the Working Class," Socialist Revolution,
Vol. 2, No. 2, March-April 1972.

Patterson, Tim. "Notes on the Historical Application of Marxist Cultural Theory," Science and
Society, Vol. 39, No. 3, Fall 1975.

Rubin, Daniel. "Communists in the McCarthy Era,"
Political Affairs, Vol. XLVIII, No. 9-10,
September-October 1969.

Sklar, Martin. "On the Proletarian Revolution and
the End of Political-Economic Society,"
Radical America, Vol. 3, No. 3, Mach-June
1969.

Weinstein, James. "The Left, Old and New,"
Socialist Revolution, Vol. 2, No. 4, July
1972.

Wolfe, Robert. "American Imperialism and the Peace Movement," Studies on the Left, Vol. 6, No. 3, May-June 1966.

Wylliams, Gwynn. "Gramsci's Concept of Egemonia," Journal of the History of Ideas, XXI, 4, Oct.-Dec. 1960.

PAMPHLETS

Gilbert, David. Consumption: Domestic Imperialism, (New England Free Press: Somerville, Mass., undated).

Haber, Barbara and Haber, Al. "Geeting by with a Little Help from our Friends," New England Free Press, 1967.

O'Brien, James. "The Development of a New Left in the United States, 1960-65," (Ph.D. dissertation, University of Wisconsin, 1971).

Perlman, Fredy. "The Incoherence of the Intellectual: C. Wright Mills' Struggle to Unite Knowledge and Action," printed by Black & Red, Detroit, 1970.

Rothstein, Richard. ERAP and How it Grew, (Boston: New England Free Press).

Rothstein, Richard. Representative Democracy in SDS, (Chicago: New University Conference, 1971).

Rothstein, Richard. "Representative Democracy in SDS," New University Conference Newsletter, Fall 1971.

Schiffrin, Andre. The Student Movement in the '50s, (New England Free Press, undated).

Students for a Democratic Society. America and the New Era, (The Wisconsin Historical Society, Madison).

Students for a Democratic Society. *The Port Huron Statement*, (Madison: Wisconsin Historical Society.

INDEX